Critical Guides to French Texts

98 Chrétien de Troyes: Perceval (Le Conte du Graal)

Critical Guides to French Texts

EDITED BY ROGER LITTLE, WOLFGANG VAN EMDEN, DAVID WILLIAMS

CHRÉTIEN DE TROYES

Perceval (Le Conte du Graal)

Keith Busby

Professor of French,
University of Oklahoma

Grant & Cutler Ltd
1993

I.S.B.N. 84-599-3329-6

DEPÓSITO LEGAL: V. 2.951-1993

Printed in Spain by
Artes Gráficas Soler, S.A., Valencia
for
GRANT & CUTLER LTD
55–57 GREAT MARLBOROUGH STREET, LONDON W1V 2AY

Contents

Preface

I would like to thank Professor Wolfgang van Emden for his constant vigilance and sound advice during the various drafts of this guide. His experience, both as a scholar of Old French and as a series editor, has been of inestimable help. Since I have taken over most of his suggestions with alacrity, I hope he will forgive me the few occasions on which I have remained recalcitrant. Thanks are also due to my former student at the University of Leiden, Marlies de Jong, for reading and commenting on an early draft from our target reader's point of view. My wife, José Lanters, read a pre-final version of the manuscript and helped remove a number of infelicities and ambiguities.

Introduction

'The life work of Chrétien de Troyes
closes on an enigma' (Per Nykrog,
69, p.267)

Perceval (or *Le Conte du Graal*) is Chrétien de Troyes's last, unfinished romance.[1] Writing in about 1225, Gerbert de Montreuil tells
us that death interrupted the poet before he was able to complete the
work (*12*, lines 6984–87). There is no reason not to believe Gerbert.
The traditional view of the period of Chrétien's literary activity —
that his first romance, *Erec et Enide*, was written about 1165, and
Perceval in the early 1180s — is the one I assume here, although
cases can be made for the period 1170–1182/83 (Fourrier, *31*) or
even 1184–1190 (Luttrell, *62*). Despite uncertainties about the
dates, it is clear that Chrétien produced five romances which played
a crucial role in the development of western fiction. It is easy to
exaggerate the importance of a single work, but *Perceval* must
assume a not inconsiderable place in literary history. Urban T.
Holmes, for example, regarded the romance as the most significant
narrative event before Dante's *Commedia* (Pickens, *73*, pp.232–33),
and *Perceval* can certainly lay an urgent claim to our attention. In
the first place, it introduces the Grail theme into literature and
opens the way for many later treatments in French and in other
languages. The potential for exploitation of the theme is created
initially by the unfinished state of the romance, which gave rise
within 50 years or so to four continuations (cf. Roach, *81*, and
Thompson, *92*). Secondly, the open-endedness of the story made it a

---

[1] All line references to *Perceval* in this study are to the edition of William
Roach, item *1* in the Bibliography at the end of this volume. Other items in
the Bibliography are referred to by an italicised number followed, where
appropriate, by a page reference.

suitable vehicle for many authors with different intentions. Finally, because its sequence of Perceval adventures is followed by an equally lengthy part concerning Gauvain, it may be the first *Doppelroman*.

Perceval differs from Chrétien's previous romances in many respects, of which the two most striking are probably the bipartite structure of the narrative and the apparent importance of religion. Yet despite the differences, it is rewarding to look at *Perceval* as part of a diversified but recognisably personal *œuvre* (cf. Kellermann, *52*, pp.7 ff.), particularly because, as Pickens suggests, the medieval audience almost certainly compared *Perceval* with 'the romance paradigm elsewhere in Chrétien' (*72*, p.33; but cf. Nykrog, *69*, p.270). *Erec et Enide*, *Cligés*, *Lancelot* and *Yvain* are by and large concerned with one central hero (and his partner) and deal with mainly secular matters, such as love between man and woman, marriage, and knighthood. All of Chrétien's poems explore different possibilities inherent in Arthurian romance, and all are to some extent experimental. It can be argued in the case of *Lancelot* that the parallel quests of the eponymous hero and Gauvain for Guenièvre contain the germ of the much more elaborate parallelism of *Perceval* (cf. Kellermann, *52*, p.15). Many other features of the poet's art and outlook familiar from other romances are clearly visible in *Perceval*, but there is little to prepare us for the introduction of the spiritual element in the form of the Grail quest, with all its implications for our view of Arthurian society. The convenient introductory survey of Chrétien's *œuvre* by Jean Frappier (*34*) will provide a more detailed context.

Perceval is the most controversial of Chrétien's romances among critics. Some interpretations appear so eccentric that William A. Nitze wrote that: 'Perhaps no work of medieval literature has suffered more from learned commentary than has the *Perceval* or *Conte del Graal*' (*68*, p.281). It has been proposed, for example, that the romance is an anti-heretical, anti-Manichean poem (Olschki, *70*), a piece of crusading propaganda (Adolf, *16*), or a detailed and symbolic Judaeo-Christian allegory (Holmes-Klenke, *48*). Olschki even suggested that *Perceval* perplexed the Middle

Ages as much as it does modern scholarship: 'The theme of the Grail and of its accompanying mysteries is without doubt the most disturbing and difficult of all the problems that medieval literature presented to contemporary readers and handed down to the curiosity of later ages' (*70*, p.1). Useful orientations in Grail literature may be found in Hoffman (*48*), Frappier (*33, 36*), and Holmes-Klenke (*48*, pp.168–94).

Perceval is the most mysterious and 'supernatural' of Chrétien's works: who is the Fisher King? What is the nature of his infirmity? What is the Grail? Why does the lance bleed? How can Gauvain possibly have found his mother and Arthur's (long since dead) in the Château des Merveilles? The questions the text poses are almost inexhaustible and Chrétien's manner of writing is such that the poem seems to suggest many things simultaneously. Instead of regarding *Perceval* as a frustrating puzzle, we should consider it a tribute to Chrétien's art that this plurality of interpretations is both possible and ultimately unsatisfactory. Ribard has aptly described all this scholarly confusion as a result of 'nos esprits rationalistes et cartésiens à la recherche d'une cohérence qui nous échappe' (*78*, p.72).

1. The Prologue

Opinion on Chrétien's prologues is divided between those who consider that they can tell us a good deal about the poet's aesthetic and the work they precede and those who consider that they cannot, but function instead as a mere *captatio benevolentiae* to gain the attention and goodwill of the audience. It would be doing a disservice to an artist like Chrétien to assume that the prologue to *Perceval* bears no relation to the rest of the text, and I therefore propose to look here at the opening 68 lines with a view to any ramifications they may have for the romance as a whole.

Chrétien's prologues show an indisputable debt to the Ciceronian rhetorical tradition (Faral, *29*; Hunt, *49, 50, 51*, and Kelly, *53*). Various rhetorical *topoi* and techniques determine their structure and functions. I disagree with Hunt in his contention that 'the content of the prologue to *Li contes del graal* is *entirely* [my italics] determined by Ciceronian moral teaching on liberality, traditional anecdotal material relating to Alexander, and fidelity to the real character of Philip of Flanders' (*49*, p.378), and that the prologue 'has nothing to offer of direct relevance to the interpretation of Perceval's chivalric and spiritual development' (*49*, p.359). The prologue's traditional rhetorical nature hardly means that it cannot also function as a preliminary indication of some of the concerns of the romance, and indeed it is typical of Chrétien's art that he should add an extra dimension to a traditional procedure (Luttrell, *63*).

Using the well-known Biblical image of reaping and sowing (II Corinthians 9:6), and further alluding to the parable of the sower (Matthew 13:3–23, Mark 4:3–20, Luke 8:5–15), Chrétien opens *Perceval* with a statement about the relationship between poet, patron, and audience. The author is the sower, casting his seed, the romance, on the fertile ground provided by the patron, in this case,

Philip of Flanders. If the seed is the romance, and if we take note of Luke 8:11, Chrétien's purpose is a lofty one indeed: 'Est autem haec parabola: semen est verbum Dei'. The seed is the word of God. A direct link is therefore suggested between the potential worth of the romance and its initial audience. Traditional flattery of the patron notwithstanding, the prologue of Chrétien's last romance resembles that of his first one, *Erec et Enide*, in that he is deeply concerned with the fate of his *œuvre*. The audience is invited to prove that it constitutes fertile ground by actively considering the meaning of the romance. Yet Chrétien's tone is not one of flattery, but of confidence and pride, and the *encomium* of Philip is enclosed by statements about the quality of the romance itself and of the *conte* on which it is based (Frappier, *34*, p.171).

In referring to his source, the *conte*, as Rupert Pickens has pointed out (61–68; *73*, p.234), Chrétien is placing his work and his own role in the tradition of *translatio*, whereby the poet is the one who translates, transmits, by means of his art the source provided by the patron. His role is therefore clearly defined at the same time that his responsibility is limited. When Chrétien states (line 8) that he is now beginning the romance, and when he ends the prologue by describing the effort he is putting into versifying the *conte*, his invitation to judge his performance (line 68) makes the audience as much witnesses to the creative process of *translatio* as critics of the finished product. The fictitious situation created is therefore one in which the poet exposes his art to an audience presided over, as it were, by the patron, who is addressed only indirectly in the third person; the audience is asked not only to judge the romance as it unfolds, but also to concur in the poet's praise of the patron. The intimate three-way relationship creates conditions conducive to the favourable and fruitful reception of the work.

Chrétien's praise of Philip is conventional, but this should not deceive us into thinking that Chrétien has nothing to say. Philip is compared favourably to Alexander the Great, a byword in the Middle Ages for virtue in general and for *largesce* (generosity) in particular. By stating Philip's superiority over Alexander, Chrétien also alludes to the *topos* of *translatio studii et imperii*, according to

which knowledge and chivalry were brought from the ancient world
to France. Philip ('… le plus preudome / Qui soit en l'empire de
Rome', 11–12) illustrates the transformation of ancient virtues into
something altogether worthier by means of their exposure to
Christianity, just as the pagan Roman Empire has been transformed
into the empire of the Church of Rome (cf. Pickens, *73*, pp.239–40).

The comparison, of course, is not merely with an historical
figure, but also, perhaps even chiefly, with a figure with a long-
standing literary reputation. From the outset, therefore, Chrétien is
presenting an amalgam of Bible, literature, and reality. The world of
the patron is the world of literature not only by virtue of the commission but also because of the comparison suggested. Philip is not
actually to become the hero of a work of literature, but his suitability
as potential hero is forcibly argued and the *encomium* intensified by
the superimposing of the literary dimension on the conventional
one.

The general theme of the prologue is charity, in the very wide
sense. *Caritas* is a favourite theme of medieval authors, and St
Augustine proposes in his *De Doctrina Christiana* that the purpose
of literature and of the study of literature is to propagate *caritas*.
Whilst the importance and universality of the Augustinian method
of reading have certainly been exaggerated, Chrétien's insistence on
charity may require us to pay more than passing attention to it. Peter
Haidu has remarked that, in Chrétien's prologue, *carité* has a three-
fold meaning: God Himself, the relationship between God and man,
and an impulse towards generosity (*43*, p.116). Augustine gives the
following definition: 'I call "charity" the motion of the soul toward
the enjoyment of God for His own sake, and the enjoyment of one's
self and one's neighbour for the sake of God; but "cupidity" is a
motion of the soul toward the enjoyment of one's self, one's neighbour, or any corporal thing for the sake of something other than
God' (original text in *14*, III 37; this translation in *15*, 3, X, 16). In
other words, *Perceval* may be about charity, about motivation and
intention, and about why people behave as they do.

The enumeration of Philip's qualities begins with a declara-
tion that he is free of Alexander's vices (16–20), a point stressed

again towards the end of the prologue: 'Ne valt cil mix que ne valut/ Alixandres, cui ne chalut/De carité ne de nul bien?' (57–59). The point is that Alexander is a hero of the ancient, pre-Christian world, and cannot therefore have known the concept of Christian charity, whatever his other virtues may have been. Charity is not defined merely in terms of giving, although Chrétien's material reward from Philip is no doubt included in it. Rather, because Philip's commission, provision of the source (line 67), and reward are all deeds carried out under the reign of charity, so is Chrétien's act of writing. This is the significance of the reference in lines 31–32 to Matthew (6:3): if the left hand is vainglory, the act of giving must be carried out with the right hand, in true charity, and concealed from the left (cf. also Topsfield, *93*, p.217). The act of writing and dissemination (sowing) is therefore inspired by charity and may be expected to be received in charity, if the soil is good. If all of these conditions are fulfilled, Chrétien's effort will not have been in vain and he may expect to reap more than he has sown. The end of the prologue neatly takes us back to the starting-point. The act of composition we are now invited to witness (line 68) is the sowing, the dissemination of the *roman*, the versified *Contes del Graal*, amongst ourselves and Philip of Flanders. The prologue may be said to fulfil two purposes: it is a statement of poetic theory and endeavour, and an introduction of themes. As the poet sows, so do his protagonists. Awareness of this dual function may inform our reading of the narrative proper.

2. The Adventures of Perceval

Perceval's Encounter with the Knights (69–363)

The narrative opens with a conventional Spring setting, but this is not (yet) a poem of courtly love, but of a widow's son in the depths of the forest. Carrying spears, the young and innocent boy, as yet unnamed, sets out to visit men working his mother's land; yet the reaction of his heart to the beauty of nature suggests a nobility of character that might not be expected in the average forest-dweller (cf. Frappier, *33*, p.79). Perceval reacts in an oddly visual way (116) to the sound of the approaching knights, and his aggressive intentions (120–24) are equally inappropriate; so too is his total reversal when they appear, as he takes them for angels led by God, the most beautiful of all. Clearly, this scene is intentionally (and successfully) humorous, but it introduces themes that are to assume a more serious function later. The most important of these themes is unquestionably that of appearance and reality, and Perceval's misapprehension is caused by his failure to interpret his mother's words any other way than literally; his dependence on his mother will also have further consequences.

The ensuing dialogue (168 ff.) is a confrontation between a representative of chivalry and one of a more natural order. In this respect, it can be compared with Calogrenant's encounter with the giant herdsman in *Yvain* (*5*, 175 ff.), where the herdsman's professed ignorance of knights and adventures provides Chrétien with a means of questioning the purpose of the knight's existence (cf. Haidu, *43*, p.118). The present interchange is a combination of misunderstanding and non-communication, as Perceval continues to take things for what they are not and persistently ignores the knight's enquiries about those he is seeking, pursuing his own single-minded set of questions. As Haidu has written: 'Here starts the comedy of two trains of thought that continually collide, and one of which is perpetually derailed' (*43*, p.122). The knight and his arms are explicable to the young *valet* only in terms of what he knows: the leader resembles God because of what his mother had told him; the lance resembles a spear and Perceval assumes it to be meant for throwing; the hauberk is seen as a potential obstacle to successful hunting; Perceval's lack of exposure to man-made objects leads him to ask whether the knight was born thus. Perceval's interrogation of the leader is interrupted by the other's impatience (231–35), and the uncouthness of Perceval is taken as illustrative of the bestial nature of the entire Welsh nation (that the story is located in Wales is only revealed in line 235, where Perceval is referred to as 'cist Galois').

When Perceval leads the knight to the harrowers (308 ff.), we learn for the first time why he was brought up in the forest: his mother had wished to conceal from him all knowledge of knights and chivalry (311–22). Since the forest is in romance the place of adventure, this may be seen as a serious misjudgement on the mother's part. The harrowers' fear that she has failed is confirmed when Perceval asks the leader of the knights where he can find the king who makes knights (322–34). Knowledge of Arthur's whereabouts is essential for the realisation of Perceval's wish to be like the knight he has just met, even though his understanding of what this means is practically non-existent. For a psychoanalytical interpretation, see Méla (*65*, p.21).

Leaving Home (364–634)

What Perceval's mother intended as protection has in fact been stifling her son, although his noble instincts now seem eventually to be coming to the fore. His absence for a few hours has plunged her into profound despair, a despair matched by the intensity of her joy at his return. His words to her are reproachful, and unintentionally blasphemous (390–94). They are also enough for her to suspect the truth, but she cannot bring herself to use the word 'chevaliers', and

has to employ a derogatory periphrasis (399–400). Indeed, her hor-
ror of the word is such that it causes her to faint when her son
pronounces it. Yet Perceval's brief experience of knights has been of
the courteous and patient kind, not the murderous and rapacious
variety his mother alludes to.

The mother now ascribes the fall of both paternal and
maternal lineages to misfortune ('mescheances', 429), whilst the
wickedness of others can by definition fall no lower than it already
is. The world is one in which virtue is no longer the guaranteed
means to continued prosperity, and in which vice is just as likely to
be rewarded. This misfortune of the family is a consequence of the
father's wound, suggestive of castration, and the prosperity of the
land is dependent on the health of the ruler (435–41); this also pre-
figures the wound of the Fisher King, to whom Perceval is related
by marriage. An additional factor in the family's misfortune is the
anarchy that reigned between the death of Uther Pendragon and the
accession of Arthur (422–49). This reference sets Perceval's family
history clearly at the beginning of the Arthurian part of Wace's *Brut*
(*13*) and is unique in Chrétien, for events in the other romances take
place at some unspecified point in the reign of Arthur (cf. Sturm-
Maddox, *91*); a parallel is suggested between Perceval's family and
that of Arthur. Furthermore, the general sense of doom that is built
up in the poem as a whole hints that the Arthurian world may be
moving towards its end. The power of this story lies not so much in
the human tragedy of a widow and bereaved mother as in the
mystery created by the vague and threatening terms in which it is
couched. What, for example, are the 'illes de mer' spoken of (419)?
How did Perceval's father come to be wounded? Who wrought the
havoc after Uther Pendragon's death? Who killed Perceval's two
brothers? Why did the crows peck out the eyes of the elder one? It is
in a sense a modern reaction to a medieval text to want all of these
mysteries solved, and Chrétien is often purposely mysterious, but
nowhere else in his *œuvre* does he use this technique to quite the
same unsettling effect. Both Frappier and Topsfield have remarked
on this allusive and impressionistic technique as being typical of
Perceval (*33*, p.67; *93*, p.212).

Chrétien pursues the idea of non-communication further by having Perceval not react to his mother's words (489–90). He merely wants to be fed and to set out to find the king who makes knights. Perceval's mother delays his departure for three days, and it is during this period that his education begins. It is also here that we may first suspect that *Perceval* is a sort of medieval *Entwicklungsroman* (Kellermann, *52*, p.20). By predicting that Arthur will respond favourably to Perceval's request for arms and by foreseeing the need for training (512–15), his mother anticipates events at court and in the house of Gornemant de Goort. The advice she now gives him is social (how to treat women (533–56), the importance of learning the name of a stranger (557–66) — we note paradoxically that Chrétien is keeping his hero's name up his sleeve) and religious (churches as places of prayer and contemplation of the crucifixion of Christ, 557–94). Given the consequences of Perceval's literal-mindedness in his encounter with the knights, the audience may well be justified in expecting further repercussions. Twice Chrétien stresses Perceval's clothing, made by his mother after the fashion of Wales (498–502; 602–03). This, with the spear and branch carried to strike the horse, ensures that, for the time being at least, Perceval will remain an innocent Welsh lad. The crudity and simplicity of the exterior matches the as yet uncultured state of the inner man.

Perceval's departure is abrupt and motivated solely by a selfish desire to obtain a shiny suit of armour. He has, as Norris J. Lacy has rightly said, mistaken the *signifiant* for the *signifié* (*58*, p.23; cf. also Pickens, *72*, p.138). He shows no interest in the fate of his father and brothers nor any concern for the feelings of his mother, and, more seriously, rides off even though he sees his mother fainting (622–25). Perceval shows a total lack of charity, though in a sense it reflects that of his mother, for the desire to stifle the feelings and inclinations of her son is at best misguided, at worst selfish and lacking in charity. The mother's attempts at cutting her son off from the world were doomed to failure because 'nobility will out'. Moreover, in his earlier romances Chrétien had made it quite

clear that human destiny must be fulfilled within society, not
without.

The Damsel in the Tent (635–833)

Just as he had mistaken the knights for God and His angels, so
Perceval, remembering his mother's description, now imagines that
the beautiful tent he finds is a church, and determines to pray in it
(655–63). Perceval's motivation is still self-interest, for whereas his
mother had said that he should worship God and pray for an
honourable life, Perceval wants to ask God to send him something
to eat (664–66). The tent turns out not to be the house of God, but of
a maiden, the subject of the other half of the mother's advice. In his
desire to follow his mother's instructions to the letter, Perceval
disregards the condition of free will (in this case, that of the
damsel), once again illustrating his lack of charitable concern for
others. Chrétien repeatedly refers to Perceval as 'niches' (681, 701),
but this is not meant to excuse his behaviour, for ignorance is no
justification for wilful disregard of the maiden's wishes. Whilst one
might dissent from Olschki's strongly doctrinaire interpretation of
Perceval as a warning against Manichean dualism, his comment on
this scene is worth quoting: 'It is here that this pure fool, without
guile or experience, appears as the victim not only of his mother's
well-intentioned advice, which he had not understood, but also of a
blind fatality that drives him towards adventure and sin' (*70*, p.7).
Perceval's addresses to the maiden are punctuated by statements of
his intention to proceed regardless: 'cui qu'il soit grief' (694);
'volsist ele ou non' (708); 'jel weil avoir' (715). His reaction to her
pleas is typically similar to his response to his mother: 'Li vallés a
son cuer ne met/Rien nule de che que il ot' (734–35); cf. 'Li vallés
entent molt petit/A che que sa mere li dist' (489–90).

When the maiden's knight returns (782 ff.), the themes of
appearance / reality and lack of communication continue to be
prominent as he takes the tracks of Perceval's *chaceor* to indicate
the recent presence of a knight and then refuses to accept her
protestations of innocence. Lack of charity in Perceval has engen-

dered lack of charity in the jealous lover, causing undeserved suffering for the tent maiden, just as Perceval had caused his mother anguish. All of the interpersonal relationships presented so far in the poem are flawed by a form of egocentrism on the part of one or more of those concerned, and in both the episode with his mother and that in the tent, the humour caused by the *niceté* of Perceval is subtended and tempered, particularly at the end of each scene, by a more serious result. We may laugh at Perceval's rustic outfit and boorish treatment of the maiden, but are disturbed by his mother's faint and the punishment inflicted by the lover (820–32).

At Arthur's Court (834–1304)

The first piece of information Perceval receives about Arthur, apart from his whereabouts, is that despite his victory over Rion des Illes he is disturbed by the departure of many of his knights for their own castles (849–58). The court of the great King Arthur, maker of knights, is thus depleted and weakened. Perceval ignores this fact, retaining only that which is relevant for his own purpose, finding Arthur. As he had earlier fixed on the idea of becoming a knight, so Perceval now determines to have the armour of the first knight he encounters. The Chevalier Vermeil's insult to Arthur and Guenièvre (889 ff.; 950 ff.) is a variant of a standard device, used in *Erec et Enide* (6, 125 ff.) and *Lancelot* (7, 31 ff.), where we actually witness the insult rather than learn of it indirectly. Again, after having told the Chevalier Vermeil that he intends to acquire his armour, Perceval ignores the aggressor's word (899) and carries on regardless.

An extraordinary sight now greets Perceval as he enters the court (discourteously, on horseback; cf. Le Rider, *60*, pp.131–32): all present are enjoying themselves except the king, lost in a depressed silence (907–11). Arguably, what is going on escapes Perceval's attention, because of his single-mindedness, but it is in any case clear that Arthur does not impress himself upon the lad by a particularly regal mien. Indeed, when Arthur is pointed out to him he cannot believe this is the maker of knights (928–30). When he finally comes to himself, Arthur cuts a pathetic figure; Guenièvre, moreover, has gone off in high dudgeon to her chamber. Arthur the king is beleaguered and depressed, and Keu the seneschal sarcastic and fractious. Arthur's finger-wagging reproach to Keu contains a piece of standard courtly advice, namely not to promise in jest that which one has no intention of giving (1009–32). In addition, he articulates what the listener knows and what the others present at court also felt on Perceval's arrival (976–78), putting his uncouthness down to an inadequate education. The presentiments about Perceval's potential now turn into predictions when the maiden laughs, thus fulfilling the earlier words of the fool (1058–62). The prophecies are, moreover, linked to the theme of Perceval's progress, as Sara Sturm-Maddox has pointed out: 'What is initiated by the prospective commentary of fool and damsel, then, is not the inevitable realization of a foretold event or series of events, but a narrative program of veridiction in which the fool's prophecy is continually tested against the hero's progressive development' (*90*, p.105). Keu knocks the damsel to the ground and kicks the fool into the fire (1048–63). Arthur's court is not a happy place to be.

The Chevalier Vermeil is waiting for 'chevalerie et aventure' (1074–75), but 'chevalerie' is the last thing that will come his way when Perceval returns. Yet again, the aggressively humorous dialogue is a model of non-communication as the two can only respond to each other's questions by repeating their own, and violence is the only way out of the verbal impasse. When the knight strikes him, Perceval reacts in the only way he knows how, by throwing a spear (1110–13). We should remember that the late twelfth century did not consider *armes de jet* an appropriate means of attack (or defence) for a knight. Apart from their evident lack of charity and chivalry, Perceval's actions after killing his opponent suggest that he treats the dead knight as if he were an animal he had killed for meat or skin. Indeed, when he comically fails to remove the armour from the dead knight, he does suggest cutting the body up into 'carbonees' as if it were a carcass (1136–38). The humour has a serious and disturbing undertone, for Perceval's selfishness, despite its cloak of endearing ingenuousness, constantly leads to suffering and death for others (cf. Topsfield, *93*, p.234).

Perceval seems to believe that the acquisition of arms and horse from the Chevalier Vermeil is the equivalent of becoming a knight (cf. lines 1134–35). The audience knows otherwise, and may be meant to interpret the lad's refusal to abandon all of his mother's clothes metaphorically: another layer must first be discarded before the real education as a knight can begin. It is also gradually becoming clearer that education is one of the romance's main concerns. We witness the hero's education directly as much of the narrative is presented through his own eyes (cf. Lacy, *58*, pp.15, 61). Line 1173 confirms that this will be a *roman d'apprentissage*, and that the *apprentissage* will not be without its trials and tribulations: 'Molt grief chose est de fol aprendre'. It is arguably at this point, clad in armour and astride the *destrier*, that Perceval begins to show his innate breeding. Despite his ignorance of stirrups and spurs, his words to Yonet might in another context be those of an accomplished knight (1193–203). And it is as a knight that Yonet refers to Perceval when delivering the cup and the message to Arthur (1213).

The words of the fool (1256–74) predict a sombre future for the Arthurian world in vague and threatening terms, and a specific and shameful fate for Keu. Sturm-Maddox (*90*, p.107) has pointed out that the scope of the prophecy has been extended from the individual fate of Perceval to that of the court as a whole. The last twenty lines or so of this section (1282 ff.) are important for their restatement of various themes and issues: Perceval is capable of being taught the art of knighthood; like Perceval's mother, Arthur fears that his lack of skill and experience will expose him to danger and even death; Arthur falls back into lamenting and regret, practically reassuming his earlier state. All in all, Arthur's court does not impose itself on the audience's consciousness as a place of sweetness, light or security. Chrétien has, as in his other romances, subverted the expectation the listener may have had of the great King Arthur's court and its inhabitants (cf., for example, Meleagant's brazen effrontery in *Lancelot* or the king's indolence at the beginning of *Yvain*).

Gornemant de Gorhaut (1305–1698)

Even though he is not yet a knight except in the most superficial of ways, Perceval — still 'li vallés' — sets out *en aventure*. Otherwise, the passage which shows Perceval arriving at the castle of Gornemant de Goort is quite unexceptional. Knights out and about come from time to time to castles where they receive hospitality and information, and there is even a sort of standard sequence of events during such episodes (Bruckner, 22). Chrétien is partly responsible both for establishing the paradigm and for introducing variations on it. The description of the landscape and the appearance to Perceval of the castle are simple but effective and prefigure his arrival at the Grail Castle (cf. Gsteiger, 42, p.13). In retrospect, it can be noted that Arthur's castle at Carduel received only the most perfunctory of descriptions (863–64), in keeping with Chrétien's apparent intention of playing down the splendour of Arthurian society. In contrast with Arthur's court, that at which Perceval now arrives is a haven of civilisation and contentment. The *preudom* who is its lord replies courteously to Perceval's greeting (1364), in contrast to Arthur's mute state. But like Arthur, the *preudom* also detects the potential beneath the surface *niceté*.

The initial dialogue reveals to the *preudom* recent events at Carduel and Perceval's misconception of what it means to be a knight. Perceval's new acquaintance also seems to be aware that things are not all they should be at Arthur's court, for he expresses surprise at the news that Arthur was able to spare the time and energy to make Perceval a knight (1371–75). The narrator, however, intervenes and declares that the romance will be no better for repetition, since the audience has already heard the tale once (1379–83). Chrétien here raises Perceval to the status of narrator and the *preudom* to that of audience. The effect is to restate the relationship sketched in the prologue between the *conte* and the act of poetic creation the audience is witnessing.

It is at this point that Perceval's real education as a knight begins; Micha (67, p.123) compares the poem as an educative work to Rabelais, Fénelon's *Télémaque*, and Rousseau's *Emile*. The *preudom*'s questions establish the rudimentary state of the lad's knowledge and each reply indicates the provenance of the knowledge, namely his mother and Yonet. Once the teacher-pupil relationship has been established (1413–18), the way is clear for the *preudom* to begin his lesson, and he succeeds where Arthur had failed, in getting Perceval to dismount (1419, cf. 979–90). The *preudom* gains Perceval's goodwill by establishing a parallel between the mother and himself (1407–09). His didactic technique is simple: providing a good example is set by the teacher, the pupil requires 'cuer et paine et us' (1467), that is to say, readiness to learn, effort and practice. Without the example to follow, the pupil cannot be blamed for ignorance (518–21; 1469–72). This recalls the mother's words in lines 516 ff., for Perceval has now found the model for emulation, and proves himself an apt pupil. *Nature* works in conjunction with *cuers* to provide *paine*; *us* then follows automatically. However, Perceval's answers to the *preudom*'s questions show that his terms of reference are still largely those of the lad brought up in the *Gaste Forest* (1530–34).

Much of the rest of Perceval's stay with the *preudom* — now revealed, thanks to the mother's advice, as Gornemant de Gorhaut — corresponds to the conventions of the hospitality sequence. In this case, the invitation to remain is not issued out of mere courtesy, but rather because Gornemant realises that Perceval still has a good deal to learn (1571–78). And Perceval's (equally conventional) refusal is motivated not by the urgency of a quest, but because he thinks back to the moment he left home and saw his mother faint. Haidu considers the desire to return to his mother 'the first sign of charity he has shown' (*43*, p.152). Before Perceval leaves, the final surface roughness is removed as Gornemant persuades him to discard the last of his mother's clothes in favour of something more suitable (1597 ff.).

The final exchanges between Perceval and Gornemant have both a ritual and didactic function. The attaching of the spur, the girding on of the sword, and the kiss complete the official initiation into knighthood, and are accompanied by a brief admonition on

the moral nature of the order and some more detailed precepts
(1624 ff.). Two of these, to aid the oppressed and to go to church to
pray for his soul, repeat advice given by his mother (in lines 532 ff.;
Perceval recognises this, lines 1672–74), but the injunction not to
talk too freely (1648–56) is new. This will have far-reaching consequences during the visit to the Grail Castle, although it is here
meant as an uncontentious piece of social advice. What Gornemant
cannot teach his pupil is not to interpret each piece of advice
literally. Now that the formation of Perceval as a knight has become
established as a main theme of the romance, his promise no longer
to refer to his mother, but rather to Gornemant, as his teacher,
confirms the change of identity from young forest-dweller to
aspirant knight. Aspirations for the future require a break with the
past, and a father-figure replaces the mother as Perceval's moral
authority (Méla, *65*, p.30). It is therefore with the filling of the void
created by the death of his father that Perceval's proper initiation
into knighthood and socialisation begins (cf. Haidu, *43*, p.154).

At Biaurepaire (1699–2975)

Perceval still largely lacks the knowledge that comes only from
experience, and we may detect a note of irony in Chrétien's description of Perceval as 'li noviax chevaliers' (1699). Upon leaving
Gornemant, Perceval heads straight for the forest, for this is still the
world he knows best, but the alternating forests and clearings of
Arthurian romance are punctuated by impressive castles, like
Arthur's and Gornemant's. However, the castle Perceval now comes
to, later (2386) said to be called Biaurepaire, is far from impressive,
but in a deplorable and dilapidated state. Perceval's entry into the
castle and the exchange between him and the maiden show little of
his previous boorishness, save a little impatience (1736–38). The
deplorable state of the land, the town and its inhabitants stands in
considerable contrast to the prosperity of Gornemant's realm.
Scarcity and plenty, infertility and fertility, poverty and prosperity,
have by now become themes of the romance: the forest that was
Perceval's home was 'gaste' (uncultivated), just like Biaurepaire

(1771); his father was wounded in the leg (the correct reading of line 436 is probably *les jambes*, which would suggest a sexual wound, echoed in the description of the Fisher King, lines 3507 ff.) and the land ruined; and Arthur's court is depopulated, weakened and exposed to attack.

Amidst the poverty and ruin lives the *châtelaine*, Blancheflor, Chrétien's description of whom (1795–829) became a classic, even in the Middle Ages. It is related to Chrétien's other descriptions of women and to the general rhetorical background of the period (cf. Colby, 25, pp.164–68). Chrétien in fact refers back to his previous works in lines 1805–09, suggesting not only that this woman is the most beautiful of all those he has ever described, but also that he is at the peak of his artistic powers. It also implies knowledge of his other romances on the part of the audience. In previous portraits, nature had been responsible for the creation of such beauty, but here the author of the wonder is said to be God Himself. The portrait is also remarkable for what it does *not* include: mouth, chin, neck, shoulders, etc., often described in other portraits; a reprise of it is found in the later scene of the three drops of blood in the snow (4197 ff.).

During the next part of the romance, we practically forget that Perceval was until very recently a boorish peasant lad, so courteous is his behaviour. Initially, his literal-mindedness causes him to sit in silence when he recalls Gornemant's advice not to talk too freely. Haidu has pointed out that the silence of this scene (1863, 1868) contrasts pointedly with Perceval's chattering to the maiden in the tent (43, p.156). The comments of the knights looking at the pair, to the effect that God made them for one another (1862–74), assume, like other remarks in the romance, the nature of a prediction (cf. Owen, 71, pp.140–41). If Perceval is learning to become a true knight, he requires inspiration for his knightly deeds which will in turn render him more worthy of love.

Perceval's telling Blancheflor about his lodgings the previous night (1884–92) ensures continuity between the episodes (as Perceval's telling Gornemant about his stay at Carduel had also done) and creates further cohesion by revealing Blancheflor as the

niece of Gornemant. Perceval's progress as a socially adept human
being can also be gauged by Blancheflor's reaction: 'Ha! biax amis,
fait la pucele, / Molt est vostre parole bele / Et molt avez dit que
cortois' (1893–95). She contrasts her own lamentable state and poor
hospitality with Gornemant's prosperity and the style in which he
had received Perceval, making explicit what the narrative sequence
had already implied. Gornemant's situation also contrasts with both
Arthur's and Blancheflor's because he is the only one of Perceval's
three hosts not beset by assailants of some kind.

Critics have discussed at length what did or did not happen
during Blancheflor's nocturnal visit to Perceval's bed (cf. Frappier,
33, pp.98–102). Certainly, the narrator's remark that all Perceval
lacked was '...le deduit/De pucele, se lui pleüst,/Et de dame, se il
leüst' (1938–40) and that he knew nothing of love may be seen as
looking forward to an occasion when Perceval *will* enjoy the fruits
of love. Although there is certainly something erotic about the scene
(Haidu, *43*, p.157), Chrétien does not insist on the matter. Whether
Perceval and Blancheflor enjoy what is often called in Old French
'le surplus' is less important than the fact that Perceval for the first
time undertakes to do something on behalf of someone else, therefore following the advice given him by both his mother and
Gornemant. Blancheflor's initiative in going to Perceval's bedside
(1954–55) is in character, stemming from the same strength of purpose that led to her breaking the ice during their earlier
conversation. Again, the word 'cortoisie' is used (1977), perhaps
not without a slight touch of irony, to describe Perceval's actions in
drawing her towards him. Although the narrator absolves
Blancheflor of any doubtful motives in coming to Perceval (1956),
although she herself protests her innocence (1986–88) and despite
the final words of her tale of woe (2035–37), there is an element of
calculation about her actions which Norris J. Lacy, rather harshly
perhaps, calls 'deviousness' (*58*, p.64). Indeed, her intentions are
now explicitly stated in lines 2040–46. Perceval's invitation to join
him in bed may simply be an innocent offer of comfort, but the
description of what takes place is purposely and playfully
ambiguous. Nevertheless, the stress on the physical proximity of the

two (2065, 2068) and the use of the word 'solas' (2067), frequent in Old French as a euphemism for sexual intercourse, indicate that Chrétien has left us to make up our own minds.

Only the morning after, when Blancheflor comes to take leave of him, does Perceval state his intention of taking up her cause (2096–106). Blancheflor's response to his request for her love if he defeats her enemy is also somewhat calculating, for she does not turn it down, merely saying that she would not want to put such a young and inexperienced knight at risk by pitting him against such a fearsome enemy (2107–24). The narrator then comments explicitly on Blancheflor's methods: because she has noticed his desire to help, she advises him against doing so to spur him on further (2128–37).

The narrative sequence of the combat between Perceval and Engygeron (2159 ff.) follows a standard pattern, from the arming of the knight to the request for mercy and the granting of it dependent on the fulfilment of a condition. In his first combat, Perceval follows to good effect the example and advice offered him by Gornemant (1473 ff., 1518 ff., 1639 ff.). Perceval has demonstrated in the last two episodes both that he has acquired a sense of charity (helping Blancheflor, granting mercy to Engygeron) and that he has made great advances in the fields of courtesy and chivalry. Uncouth and boorish behaviour no longer characterises his social contacts; on the contrary, both narrator and other characters express approval of his actions. Engygeron remarks: 'Chevaliers voir es tu molt buens' (2248), but also that his own reputation is such that Perceval would not be believed if he said he had defeated him. He then offers to go and announce the defeat himself so as to render it credible (2248–59). This illustrates the importance of reputation in the Arthurian world, and relates to the mother's dictum that a man is known by his name, for without an accumulated reputation, a man has no identity. Perceval, as a beginning knight, has no reputation and, significantly, no name as yet.

Only on the third occasion does Engygeron agree to present himself to a person of Perceval's choosing. The further stipulation that Engygeron also transmit a message to the maiden who had laughed provides a structural link back to a previous part of the narrative (2313–25). Two points need to be made here. Firstly, despite the rules and conventions of courtesy and chivalry, Arthurian society is riddled with family feuds and hatred between members of particular lineages, and the world outside the confines of courts and castles seems to be one of anarchy and violence. Secondly, in addition to stressing the enmity of Engygeron with Blancheflor and Gornemant, Perceval's first two suggestions betray his still incomplete knowledge of how things should be done, as the traditional procedure in Arthurian romance is to send the defeated opponents straight back to Arthur's court. This is one of the channels by means of which news is transmitted, and in this particular case it is also necessary for thematic and narrative purposes, constituting one of Perceval's few points of contact with Arthur.

In justifying his refusal to behead his defeated opponent, Perceval now repeats Gornemant's advice (1643–47; 2348–50) in much the same way as he used to repeat his mother's. The communal joy at Perceval's achievement is then suitably expressed in personal fashion by Blancheflor. At the same time that Perceval returns to Biaurepaire and Engygeron heads for Arthur's court, the latter's lord, Clamadeu, moves towards Biaurepaire in the belief that it is now his (2363–65). The information he receives from a *valet* serves again to summarise recent events and to mark Perceval now as the Chevalier Vermeil. The transformation now seems complete: the self-centred *nice* has become the knight inspired by love to great deeds of prowess in the service of others. All that he still lacks is a name.

Despite Perceval's victory over Engygeron, the situation still seems desperate for the inhabitants of Biaurepaire when Clamadeu is persuaded by one of his knights to try to starve them into surrender (2401 ff.). This plan, however, is undermined by the fortuitous arrival at Biaurepaire of a ship full of provisions, blown off course (2524 ff.). The actual practical details of selling and buying food are rarely shown in romance, and Chrétien's treatment of the merchants and the general welcome afforded them has been taken to suggest that not only did he approve of the activity, but also that he may have had at least a partial eye on an eventual bourgeois audience. Clamadeu's enraged reaction to the good fortune of Biaurepaire, in what Kellermann (*52*, p.127) sees as one of Chrétien's touches of psychological realism, is to challenge Perceval to a single combat (2593–99). Perceval's defeat of Clamadeu follows a pattern similar to that of Engygeron, for he, too, refuses to surrender to Blancheflor or Gornemant, agreeing to go to Arthur's court with the same message for the damsel (2684–99).

The arrival of Clamadeu at Arthur's court quickly follows that of Engygeron, thereby giving a concentrated boost to the reputation of Perceval (cf. Bezzola, *19*, p.19). The description of Keu here (2793–817) is particularly interesting as it shows a contrast between his outer beauty and his malicious tongue, reintroducing the theme of appearance and reality. Quite frequently in romance, Arthur refuses to eat until news arrives at court or some marvellous event takes place. The refusal, as here, is always a narrative indication that the desired condition is about to be met. Chrétien has avoided repetition by describing in detail only the nature of Clamadeu's arrival and the exchanges between him and Arthur, allotting only a few lines to the earlier arrival of Engygeron. Clamadeu's flattery of Arthur's reputation (2831 ff.) may seem in stark contrast with the latter's own performance in this particular romance. The customary blame of Keu (2878–81) can now been seen in the light of Gornemant's advice to Perceval (1648–56), for if Keu had been capable of holding his slanderous tongue, Arthur would not have lost Perceval. Like Engygeron, Clamadeu is pardoned and retained by Arthur as a member of his household (2908–09). This is also standard practice in the romance, for the court functions not only as a *point de repère* whence knights depart and whither they return, and whither prisoners are sent to surrender, but it also absorbs all those it can. All of Chrétien's previous romances show a desire to integrate the heroes into the court, in spite of which there seems to be a progressive breaking away from it. In the unfinished romance as we have it, Perceval is never properly integrated into the fabric of Arthurian society and the court goes to considerable lengths to try to bring him back.

In Biaurepaire, Perceval is offered the lordship of the land which would entail marriage with Blancheflor, now described as his *amie* (2912, 2935), a word with deeper and more permanent connotations than in modern French. Perceval in principle accepts the offer, but must first ascertain the truth about his mother, for the image of her falling in a faint seems to haunt his memory (2917–19). Perceval is now torn between two worlds, the old one of the Gaste Forest where he grew up with only his mother and a few servants for company, and the new one of Arthur, Gornemant, and above all, Blancheflor, through which he now moves with consummate ease. His parting words and promises to the inhabitants of Biaurepaire make it clear that he is afraid of what might have happened when he left, but that he is determined to integrate his mother, alive or dead, into Biaurepaire, to integrate the old world with the new (2926–37). His departure is accompanied by the conventional attempts at dissuasion. The nuns and monks, who were respectively 'esbahies' and 'esgarez' (1758–59) and silent when Perceval arrived in the run-down Biaurepaire, have found their voices at the same time that the town is restored to prosperity.

Perceval at the Grail Castle (2976–3421)

After Perceval left his mother's house, he had been able to think of nothing but becoming a knight. Upon his departure from Biaurepaire he begins to relate everything he sees to the task of finding his mother again. That strange things may be about to occur is indicated in lines 2976–79, and indeed, the purely rational events of the narrative so far begin to be replaced by vaguely mysterious and unsettling occurrences. The river looks like an insurmountable barrier to progress, and although his prayer (2990–93) seems to be answered by the appearance of the boat, the fisherman offers little comfort, only immediate hospitality. Olschki writes that the river 'marks the entrance to the kingdom of mystery which is not always subject to the clarity and logic that are generally characteristic of Chrétien's lucid style and invention' (*70*, p.7). Chrétien does not actually say that Perceval crosses the river, but everything now happens as though he is in the other world. Chrétien may simply not have included one detail of his source.

After the sojourns with Gornemant and Blancheflor, the fisherman's (3026–34) is the third offer of shelter that Perceval receives, yet from the beginning there is something strange about it, for the encounter of the hero with a fisherman in a boat is unusual. Even though the appearance of a castle out of nowhere cannot be shown to be a supernatural occurrence in the strict sense of the word, it does have a startling suddenness (3050–51), again probably attributable to an ultimately Celtic source. Jean Frappier (*35*) and Maurice Delbouille (*27*) debated the matter in great detail but without settling the issue definitively, largely because Chrétien's text does not allow a definite conclusion to be drawn. Perceval's frustration at not being able to find the fisherman's home (3040–49; another one of the moments of psychological realism noted by Kellermann, *52*, p.127) leads to a temporary relapse into uncharitable impetuosity, of which, however, he immediately repents. The effect is somewhat comic, rather like that of the sudden metamorphosis of the devils into angels in lines 111 ff.

What characterises this episode generally is an alternation of the normal and the abnormal. Perceval's approach to the castle is unconventional by virtue of the fisherman and the sudden appearance of the castle, but convention and reassurance seem to return as he crosses the bridge into the building itself. The description of the hall with its fire and chimney and columns — perhaps exceptional for the late twelfth century — is extensive, and the position of the host on a bed suggests something unusual (3082 ff.). The host himself explains that his inability to rise is due to his infirmity, but no further details are given here. The attentive listener may have associated the Fisher King's wound described in lines 3512 ff. with that which led to the death of Perceval's father, in which case the host may be seen as a vision of the absent father (cf. Fowler, *32*, p.30), which association would provide more support for the psychoanalytical interpretation of Méla. On a less speculative level, Perceval still does not seem to have developed the habit of sympathising fully with those in distress; this is indicated by his reaction to the host's apology, which is expressed in purely self-oriented terms (3110–12). It is, of course, the host, not Perceval, who stands in need of happiness and good health. As Perceval had explained to Gornemant that he had come from Arthur's court, and to Blancheflor that he had come from Gornemant's, he now tells his host that he left Biaurepaire only that morning (3122–23). The host's reaction in lines 3124–27 — that Perceval must have arisen early to have come so far — is a perfectly rational one, banal even, and gives no indication of the nature of the events Perceval is about to witness.

The sword sent as a present by the host's niece is a mysterious object, both with respect to its provenance and destiny (3130 ff.). The invalid host is apparently aware of his guest's identity, but the nature and source of his knowledge are nowhere explained. Although the sword is a sign of election (cf. Frappier, *33*, p.112), Le Rider has pointed out that the fact that it will break as soon as Perceval tries to use it may be suggestive of his failure in the Grail Castle as a whole (*60*, p.76). What lends this episode its particular tone is the contrast between the slightly awkward and humorous conversation and the intimation of a great destiny (cf. Haidu, *43*, p.171). More mysterious still is the procession that follows (3190 ff.). It is true that the Perceval-adventures often depend for their effect on the discrepancy between what the audience knows and what Perceval knows. In the case of the Grail procession, however, the audience is as ignorant as the hero, whence the sense of mystery and curiosity. During the whole of this cortège, Perceval remains silent, remembering Gornemant's advice (1648–56), and the narrator implies that Perceval's following the advice rather than his own inclinations may have harmful consequences (3248–51). Certainly, Perceval's failure to satisfy his own curiosity fires that of the audience in a rare moment of empathy. A conventional hospitality sequence is then resumed, but the table-top and trestles are unusual in that they are of ivory and ebony respectively, and stand out by virtue of their richness. With the serving of the meal, the fantastic and the natural combine, for the haunch of venison *au poivre*, a standard medieval dish, is cut on the silver platter that had just formed part of the mysterious procession. The narrator again attributes Perceval's silence at the passing of the Grail to adherence to Gornemant's advice (3204–09; 3294–97). As Norris J. Lacy says, it is possible to see here a theme common in Chrétien's *œuvre* as a whole, namely the 'conflict between a character's natural (and therefore good) impulse and the action dictated by an artificial and learned code of behaviour' (*58*, p.5). This is especially plausible in the light of the narrator's repeated suggestion of Perceval's failure and its consequences (3298).

The alternation between the conventional and the mysterious continues with the disappearance of the Grail and the resumption of the meal (3310 ff.). As with the table-top and trestles, there is more than a hint of the luxurious and exotic in the list of wines, fruits and spices served. When Perceval wakes up the next morning, the mysterious atmosphere dominates again, for the castle is deserted (3359–60), his horse ready saddled (3380), and the drawbridge already down (3387). Faced with this enigma, Perceval devises a rational explanation, concluding that the servants must have gone into the forest to inspect traps (3392–95). He intends to follow them to ask why the lance bleeds and whither the Grail is carried, but as he rides out, the drawbridge suddenly closes, requiring him to jump to safety ('the courtly equivalent to farce's kick in the pants', Haidu, *43*, p.175). Despite his *charité* in the Biaurepaire episode, it can be argued that Perceval has failed to demonstrate that virtue here and has missed the point of what the audience knows to have been a test. The test, however, was of a fundamentally different nature from those he had met before, for it required him to go beyond the veil of appearances by means of some form of intuition or grace (cf. Frappier, *33*, p.117). Frustrated curiosity, not sympathy for the still wounded Fisher King, is the emotion he shows when leaving the Grail Castle (cf. Le Rider, *60*, p.91).

I have no intention of offering a detailed commentary and 'explanation' of the events at the Grail Castle. These scenes have caused more ink to flow than any other part of Chrétien's *œuvre*, and all attempts to offer a consistent and logical interpretation have failed. The reason for this is that Chrétien is being purposefully

mysterious and knows that the best method of sustaining the atmosphere is to avoid extremes of the supernatural, for if we assume
that the Grail was carried and did not move of its own accord, the
only aspect of the scene that cannot be explained in terms of the
laws of physics is the Bleeding Lance. 'L'effet du graal n'a rien de
spécial — ce n'est qu'un plat', wrote Bezzola (*19*, p.48). Research
has in fact shown that the word *graal* is derived from Latin *gradale*,
meaning a large dish used to serve food at various stages of a meal,
and that it is attested (though not frequently) in Old French as a
common noun in that sense (cf. Frappier, *33*, pp.5–12, and Roques,
82).

The researches of Jean Marx and R.S. Loomis plausibly argue
for the Celtic mythological origin of the episode and the Grail story
as a whole, but say little about *Perceval* as a piece of literature
(Marx, *64*; Loomis, *61*). This theory of Celtic origins (which
Loomis also applied to Chrétien's other works) maintains that
Chrétien began the process of Christianising an originally pagan
Celtic cauldron of plenty (cf. Loomis, *61*). Olschki's view of the
Grail Castle as a den of heretics is exaggerated, but as Pierre Gallais
has said (*41*, p.479), it may indicate that Chrétien alludes to certain
heretical movements of his day of which his patron, Philip of
Flanders, was a sworn enemy. Moreover, even in general terms,
Olschki's comments about the maimed king add a spiritual dimension to the romance: 'He is injured in his virility which lies at the
root of all sin' (*70*, p.34). The pun on *pescheor* (fisherman) and
pecheor (sinner) is thus seen as pointing to the meaning of the
poem as a whole. Given Philip's crusading activities, Helen Adolf's
opinion that the Grail Castle is to be taken as the Holy City or the
Holy Sepulchre and the Fisher King as the Leper King of Jerusalem,
Baldwin, may also represent a set of contemporary associations, but
not a key to unlocking the poem as a whole as a piece of crusading
propaganda (*16*). The solemnity of the procession is suggestive of
the liturgy, particularly the Byzantine rite (Anitschkof, *17*), and the
bleeding lance suggests the Holy Spear that pierced the side of the
crucified Christ, but this does not tell us very much about what
Chrétien may have been trying to do or say. Few scholars have

espoused the interpretation of Holmes and Klenke, according to which the Grail Castle is a representation of the Temple of Solomon, the Fisher King Jacob (and by extension, the Jewish people), and the basic idea of the poem 'the conversion of the Old Testament into the New — Solomon's Temple into Ecclesia' (*48*, p.77). One of the fundamental flaws in these theories is that they all but ignore the Gauvain-part of the romance and base their findings on approximately half of the extant text. Attempts to 'unlock' *Perceval* (cf. the 'Alphabetical Key to the Symbolism of Chrétien's *Perceval*', *48*, pp.195–214) tend to ignore both the poetry and the consequences of Chrétien's use of mythical material (cf. Poirion, *74*, p.196).

The entire episode is masterfully executed and carefully related to earlier parts of the romance. Perceval arrives at the Grail Castle thinking of his mother (2980–84); his stay with Gornemant is woven into the fabric by virtue of the consequences of the advice not to talk too freely (3204–09; 3294–97). As he leaves the Grail Castle, therefore, two major problems remain unsolved for him, that of the nature of the Grail procession and its constituent elements, and the fate of his mother. The following episode will provide revelations on both.

Perceval and his Cousin (3422–3690)

Nothing could be more commonplace in Arthurian romance than the hero meeting a damsel lamenting the death of her lover, wishing that she herself were dead. But what begins traditionally diverges from the standard pattern when the damsel cuts short her answer to Perceval's question about who killed the knight in order to remark on the surprisingly healthy state of both Perceval and his mount (3466–82). This not only serves to contrast rather obviously her grief and Perceval's well-being, but is also disorienting because it is psychologically inconsistent: damsels lamenting the death of their lovers do not usually bother themselves very much about other people's horses. The damsel realises that the Fisher King's residence is the only place Perceval could have come from

(3494–95). The ensuing dialogue fulfils a number of functions, chief amongst which are the narrative recapitulation (which occurs at the beginning of practically every section) and the explanation, *post eventum*, of recent happenings (cf. Kellermann, *52*, p.44). The similarity between the wound of the Fisher King (3509–15) and that of Perceval's father (435–41) is suggestive, and like the latter, the Fisher King has had a house built to which to retire, indulging in the only pastime of which he is now capable. The damsel's series of staccato questions (3557 ff.) enables her to ascertain that Perceval has failed the test.

Kellermann has shown (*52*, pp.60–83) how *retardatio* is frequently used by Chrétien to create and maintain suspense, often revealing the hero's name only well into the romance (*Lancelot* is another obvious example), for despite my referring for the sake of convenience to Perceval by his name during this commentary, it must be remembered that it is first mentioned in line 3575. Perceval's guessing his name is a moment of revelation and self-awareness, and its delayed first mention cannot be explained away by simply saying, as does Peter Haidu, that no-one had asked it before (*43*, p.180). Bezzola suggests that the guess amounts to Perceval's realisation of his destiny, for 'tout nom comporte une mission' (*19*, p.58). For Frappier, it is, less mystically, Perceval's becoming aware of his own personality (*33*, p.121). It occurs at the moment that the nature of his errors is pointed out to him, for although he had acquired both the outer and some of the inner qualities of a knight, he lacked that which gives a man his identity, his name. Yet Perceval's existence as *Perchevax li Galois* is a short one, for whilst his guess lends him an identity by virtue of his geographical provenance, his cousin substitutes another epithet which has its origin in his two errors (3582). The significance of Perceval's silence at the Grail Castle is now clarified, and the similarity between the Fisher King and Perceval's father is confirmed by the link now established between the wound and the prosperity of the kingdom. Structurally, the failure is linked to an earlier part of the romance by the attribution of his silence to the sin he incurred by causing the death of his mother. Perceval's proud announcement that not a word escaped his lips (3570) refers to Gornemant's advice, but the damsel's deflating reaction (3571) comes from her realisation of his sin. The revelations continue with a sketch of a network of family relationships, for the sorrowing maiden is Perceval's cousin (3596–601). The misadventures of Perceval are then linked by his cousin to the death of her *ami*, and an impression of fatality is created by her constant use of words such as 'mal aventurous' (3584), 'avenist' (3590), 'avenront' (3592), 'mescheü' (3603). Misfortune occurs, befalls, and frequently affects those who have apparently done nothing to deserve it; this seems to have been the case with Perceval's father, the maiden of the tent, Blancheflor, the Fisher King, and Perceval's cousin herself. Yet Perceval's misfortune is attributed to *pechié* (3593), which he is unaware of having committed. It is explicable in terms of his earlier lack of charity which was beginning to impinge on his conscience, and which has obviously not yet been redeemed by his charitable actions since leaving Gornemant de Gorhaut. We should also note the cousin's switching from *vous* to *tu* when Perceval's *pechié* is revealed (3581 ff.); the change is certainly deliberate on Chrétien's part, reflecting the cousin's respect turning to contempt.

The cousin's reproach and the news of his mother's death shake Perceval into an awareness of past and future of the consequences of what he has done and of his responsibility for others. Learning of his mother's death is another turning-point in the narrative, for his quest to find her is now necessarily at an end, and he realises that he must take another path (3622–25). There are at this point two matters outstanding, namely the situation of the Fisher King and the avenging of his cousin's *ami*. Perceval chooses the latter. Arguably, there is a kind of unintentional brutality about Perceval's brushing aside his cousin's grief with a proverb (3630); the brutality is the kind we have noted elsewhere (cf. Hoggan, 47, p.269). The cousin also mysteriously knows things, such as the provenance of the sword given to Perceval, and she repeats (3654–63) the prediction about its breaking, first suggested in the description of the sword itself (3138–43). The passage again

summarises events at the Grail Castle and elucidates mysteries
associated with them.

Perceval and the Orgueilleux de la Lande (3691–4143)

Perceval leaves one sorrowing maiden only to encounter another,
but one he has seen before in quite a different state. The maiden is
in a condition comparable to that of her wretched mount, and
Chrétien is using the conventional description of maiden and
palfrey, reversing some of the elements so as to create not so much a
parody as a pathetic picture of animal and human neglect
(3695–747). A contrast is surely intended with Perceval and his
horse at the beginning of the previous episode. Wolfgang Brand has
examined the use of repetition and contrast in Chrétien's *œuvre* and
shown how extremely varied and subtle it is in *Perceval*. The case
of the two sorrowing maidens is one example; interplay between the
Perceval and the Gauvain adventures adds another dimension to the
technique (Brand, *21, passim*; cf. also Kellermann, *52*, pp.54–60).
As with Chrétien's portrait of Enide, this maiden's dress matches
her mental and physical state. Her nipples, which in the portrait of
conventional beauty are enticingly visible beneath the dress, are
here exposed by the holes in it (3722–23). The skin, usually white
and soft to the touch, is rough and lacerated from exposure to all
weathers (3726–29). Descriptions of the face usually stress the
rosiness of cheeks on white skin, but here the marks left by tears are
alone visible (3731–34). The audience may already have linked this
description to the punishment inflicted by her *ami* on the Maiden of
the Tent (822–32).

The previous scene had related to recent events in the Grail
Castle, but this one shows a somewhat more distant and less charitable past catching up with Perceval. The two characters do not recog-
nise each other, but she is revealed as the damsel he had kissed in
the tent. Their second meeting is quite different from the first, and
Perceval's interest has this time been awakened by a charitable
sense of pity rather than by the foolish desire for the ring and a kiss.
For a second time, Perceval is reproached with *pechiez* by a damsel,

although it is not clear what the *pechiez* (3810) is supposed to refer to. It seems that Perceval has found his immediate objective, for the knight, called the Orgueilleux de la Lande, is the one who had killed his cousin's *ami*. When the Orgueilleux returns from the woods (as he had done in the earlier episode), he relates to Perceval the events in the tent in which Perceval himself had been one of the chief participants (635 ff.). The story of the Orgueilleux not only summarises earlier events, sometimes approaching verbatim quotation (822 ff., cf. 3890–98), but also puts the story from the point of view of someone for whom Perceval is still 'uns vallés galois' (3850). Although the beginning of the Orgueilleux's speech makes it plain that he genuinely loved the damsel (3848), the rest of it turns into an anti-feminist tirade in an established medieval tradition (3863–75); such sentiments are relatively rare in Chrétien's work. Frappier has also pointed out (*33*, pp.128–29) that this is the only occasion in his entire *œuvre* that Chrétien depicts a jealous lover; when he does so, however, it is one unbalanced by the disturbing intensity of his passions. What we have here is a mixture of narrative summary and anti-feminism once more illustrating the lack of charity that determines the behaviour of many of the characters. It is given an added piquancy here by the fact that the Orgueilleux is unaware for the time being that he is addressing the supposed miscreant from the tent. Inability to communicate frequently arises from an attitude that disposes one character never to believe, or even listen to, what another says. Instances of Perceval not listening are legion at the beginning of the romance, and both episodes concerning Perceval, the Orgueilleux, and his damsel are marked by the failure to communicate. Not only does the Orgueilleux refuse to believe the damsel, but he now refuses to believe Perceval's truthful version of events, preferring the one born in his own uncharitable and fevered imagination (3911–13). The lack of verbal communication inevitably leads to physical combat.

By his victory over the Orgueilleux, Perceval redeems his own earlier uncharitable treatment of the damsel, and forces the Orgueilleux to do likewise. The message he is instructed to deliver to Arthur is identical to that already delivered by Engygeron and

Clamadeu: that Perceval will not return to Arthur's court before having avenged the maiden who smiled at him (2321–23, 2694–99, 3976–80). The confession of defeated knights in front of the court is a ritual that cleanses their conscience and renders them fit to be absorbed into the ranks of Arthur's men. As the knight is presented to Arthur, so the *amie* is presented to Guenièvre, becoming one of her *puceles* (4050–53). Gauvain, who had not been at court during Perceval's brief visit, wonders who the knight can be (4086–95). This requires and enables Chrétien once more to summarise earlier events, on this occasion Perceval's first visit to court and how he acquired the arms of the Chevalier Vermeil (4096 ff.). The court's determination to set out after Perceval underlines not only his stature now, but also the eagerness with which Arthur seeks to absorb into his household all those who can add lustre and fame to it. This will eventually lead to a reunion of hero and Arthurian court. Arthur's words to Gauvain therefore fulfil a double function: they constitute part of the periodic recapitulation of events, refreshing the memory and at the same time extending the potential of the narrative into the future.

The Drops of Blood on the Snow (4144–4602)

On this occasion, Arthur's vow to find Perceval is to be fulfilled almost immediately. The description of Arthur's departure from Carlion and setting up camp is followed straightaway by a return to Perceval, now in the vicinity (4164). The grand style of the court's setting out contributes to a sense of anticlimax when the journey is cut short. The scene of Perceval's reverie before the three drops of blood on the snow is one of Chrétien's most memorable and most successful pieces, according to Frappier (*33*, p.130), 'le plus poétique', and is worth looking at in some detail. Perceval is now involved in truly knightly activities:

> Et Perchevax la matinee
> Fu levez si come il soloit,

> Que querre et encontrer voloit
> Aventure et chevalerie. (4164–67)

The worldly connotations of the terms used may indicate, however,
that Perceval's chivalry is still lacking a spiritùal, charitable,
dimension. A stark white backdrop is created by the cold and snow,
against which the blood of the goose is spilled. The success of the
scene lies in its powerful evocativeness. First and foremost, it relates
to Perceval's love for Blancheflor and leads directly to his trance. It
is also suggestive of an intuitive love, not the reasoned and intel-
lectual kind we sometimes find in medieval literature and elsewhere
in Chrétien's own work (*Cligés* (*4*), 575 ff., 2956 ff. would be the
most evident example). The symbolism of the blood is here
multivalent, for line 4187 in particular reminds us of the bleeding
lance of the Grail Castle (3192–201); it is tempting, too, to see the
falcon as a male symbol and the goose as the female, the encounter
between the two evoking the first sexual act between Perceval and
the maiden Blancheflor. Blood and the colour red are generally used
to good effect in *Perceval*: Perceval kills the Chevalier Vermeil and
dons red armour himself (1076 ff.); the defeated Clamadeu arrives
at Arthur's court covered in blood (2773), the lance of the Grail
procession bleeds, etc. (cf. Potters, *77*). For Perceval, however, the
blood and snow are associated with Blancheflor alone, not the lance
(cf. Pickens, *72*, pp.256–57). The present scene is a very literary
one, for red on white is an almost indispensable element of the
standard female portrait, prescribed by rhetoricians such as Geoffrey
of Vinsauf (cf. Colby, *25*, pp.92 ff.). Indeed, line 4204, 'Li vermels
sor le blanc assis', reproduces verbatim line 1824, where it had been
part of the portrait of Blancheflor (note that the rhyme *en/sor son
vis* is also repeated in lines 4203 and 1823). Interestingly, the
portrait of Blancheflor picks up here where the earlier one
(1795–829) had left off. The love-trance, too, is traditional, and
Chrétien himself had used it elsewhere, particularly in *Lancelot*; the
vocabulary of the scene is also that of 'courtly love': 's'oblie'
(4202), 's'amie bele' (4210), 'muse' (4211), etc. (cf. Frappier, *33*,
pp.138–39). Daniel Poirion writes of this scene: 'Le Moyen Age ne

connaît pas l'inconscient freudien. Mais il connaît le rêve, l'extase, et ce qu'il appelle l'*entr'oubli*. On ne peut refuser à l'auteur ce qu'il accorde à Lancelot, à Yvain, à Perceval: un type de pensée qui se laisse envahir par l'imagination. La poétique de Chrétien de Troyes ici a l'art de nous faire rêver' (75, pp.153–54).

The practical result of the trance is to render Perceval immobile long enough to enable the court to make an attempt to contact him. At Arthur's command, Sagremor attempts to persuade Perceval to return to the camp, but audience expectation, aroused at least partly by the epithet 'li Desreez' (4221, 'the impetuous'), is met when Sagremor's impatience and gruffness cause Perceval to emerge from his reverie long enough to unhorse him. Here, values are reversed, for the wild lad from the woods is the embodiment of courtly emotions whilst a member of the most famous court of the earth shows a lack of courtesy and consideration. Keu's approach and subsequent failure are fundamentally the same as Sagremor's, and one notes in both encounters the recurrence of phrases such as 'mal gre vostre' (4250), 'mal gre suen' (4279), or 'ou il weille ou non' (4287) and threats of dire consequences if Perceval does not comply (4297). Again, all revolves around matters of speaking and listening: Sagremor speaks (4244), Perceval remains silent (4248); Sagremor has wasted his breath (4252–53), so he shouts (4258), and Perceval finally reacts (4260–62); Keu shouts (4294) and Perceval hears himself threatened (4299). When communication is achieved, the message is one of aggression leading to conflict.

Keu's defeat by Perceval fulfils the fool's prediction about the dislocated shoulder (1260 ff.). If we tend to dismiss unhorsing as a mere result of defeat, we should remember that the horse lends the knight his identity; to be unhorsed is not only to be defeated, but also to be despoiled of an indispensable attribute of the profession.

Perceval has surpassed Sagremor and Keu in courtesy and prowess, but he has not yet pitted himself against the yardstick of knightly achievement, Gauvain. Here is a concrete example of what Kellermann discerned as a major theme of *Perceval*: 'Höfisches Sein im Gegensatz zu dem Werdeprozess' ('Courtly existence versus development', 52, p.27). In the light of a particular narrative sequence from *Erec et Enide* (*6*, 3928 ff.), where Gauvain succeeds in bringing Erec back to camp where Keu had failed, the audience may have been expecting Gauvain to go and bring Perceval back. Before this, however, there is an interesting exchange between Gauvain and Keu (4349–412). Gauvain's comments on Perceval's trance are what we would expect from the embodiment of courtesy, and he even has an idea of what is causing the trance (4360–63). He proposes *to ask* Perceval to return to the camp (4368–69), not order and threaten him as the other two had done. The speech is, in short, a model of reason, moderation, consideration, and perhaps even charity. Keu, however, sees it as a piece of rhetoric (which, of course, it is), predicts that it will work, and that Gauvain will convince Perceval to return by virtue of being a smooth talker winning over someone tired out by two combats and in no fit state to resist (4371–403). Keu's own words also constitute a piece of rhetoric, the complexity of which belies the apparently simple sarcasm (cf. Haidu, *43*, pp.194–95). Yet the sarcastic statement can also be taken literally, and the audience may suspect that sarcasm masks the truth. Keu's insinuation is that in Gauvain the polish of courtesy has replaced the substance, making it empty, unassertive flattery. Gauvain replies to Keu as 'biax dols amis' (4409), although his response is not without its own sarcasm.

The meeting between Gauvain and Perceval is crucial, for here the most accomplished of Arthur's knights (4419–20) meets one destined to surpass him, if the earlier words of the damsel and the fool are to be believed (1039–44; 1059–62). Any suspicions harboured about the truth behind Keu's sarcasm are reinforced when Chrétien says that the drops of blood had been almost completely absorbed by the snow (4426–29); Perceval's trance is less deep and Gauvain's task easier. Gauvain's approach is not only courteous, but contrasted with those of Sagremor and Keu: he approaches at a gentle trot (4433; instead of at a gallop), without threatening (4434; Sagremor grew angry, Keu shouted), and addresses Perceval politely, requesting him to come and talk to Arthur (4439–41; both Sagremor and Keu had said Perceval must come, like it or not). The consummate courtesy of Perceval's trance

is now authenticated by the great Gauvain, who also condemns the
boorishness of the two previous ambassadors (4457–61). Gauvain
does not forget the mission he is on, however, and his next words,
despite the piling up of conditionals, repeat the earlier sentiment
voiced, albeit more crudely, by Sagremor and Keu (4462–65).
Perceval, recognised by Gauvain from his comments about Keu,
earns esteem by virtue of his reputation before the revelation of his
name; on the other hand, Gauvain first reveals his own name, which
is then associated by Perceval with the reputation of Arthur's
famous nephew (4488–89). It should also be noted that this is the
second time (4483) that Perceval states his name. On the first
occasion he has called himself 'li Galois' (3575), but his cousin had
transformed it immediately into 'Perchevax li chaitis' (3582). The
effect of his naming himself now is to enable the world to attach a
name to the reputation, for, as his mother said: 'Par le sornon
connoist on l'ome' (562). The wild young Welsh lad from the forest
now meets the great Gauvain, nephew of King Arthur, on equal
terms. The sight of Gauvain returning with Perceval draws a further
sarcastic comment from Keu (4518–31). However, the narrator is
careful not to divest Keu of all credibility, and leaves all possibilities
open by his 'Einsi dist Kex, soit drois ou tors' (4532). There is also
a certain pomp, perhaps even pompousness, in the way Gauvain
prepares Perceval for the meeting with Arthur, giving him some of
his own clothes, and going hand-in-hand with his new acquaintance
to the king. The presentation itself is rhetorical and flowery ('Je vos
amain.../Celui que vos.../.../C'est cil.../C'est cil.../Je le vos bail,
veez le chi', 4546–53). As Frappier has written: 'Si la destinée de
Perceval était seulement d'égaler un Gauvain, l'histoire pourrait
s'arrêter là. Mais il n'en est rien' (*33*, p.141).

The Hideous Damsel (4603–4815)

The joy at the reunion with Perceval is short-lived and dampened by
the arrival of the Hideous Damsel. In the world of romance, there is
nothing particularly unusual about a damsel on a mule arriving at
Arthur's court to deliver a message, but from our first glimpse of

this one it is clear that Chrétien is confronting us with a variation on the traditional paradigm. Her ugliness is such that the narrator himself, by referring to his source (the same book that Philip had given him), expresses scepticism as to whether she can really be as ugly as she is supposed to be (4616–19). Her portrait is a parody by inversion of the traditional female portrait: her tresses are black, whereas they ought to be as yellow as gold; there is nothing as ugly, even in hell, whereas poets usually express admiration of God's handiwork; her neck and hands are black, whereas they ought to be as white as alabaster; her eyes are like rat's eyes, whereas they are usually like those of a falcon; her lips are as large as those of an ass or a cow, whereas they ought to be small and round; her teeth are discoloured yellow and red, whereas they should be pure white; her chest protrudes like a hunched back, whereas she should have small, round breasts; and so on. The description of the lower parts of the body are as evocative of sexual disgust as those in the traditional portrait are of pleasure (4633–37). In fact, parts of this portrait are such clear inversions of details in the portrait of Blancheflor that comparison may be invited. The arrival of the Demoiselle Hideuse, at the height of Perceval's glory, closely resembles that of Laudine's messenger in *Yvain* (5, 2704 ff.), and there are even verbatim similarities (*Yvain* 2716–18, cf. *Perceval* 4642–44).

The usual function of the damsel on the mule is to set the narrative going by causing the knights to depart from court (someone needs avenging, defending, rescuing, etc.). The function of this scene, however, is more than that. It constitutes the second reproach Perceval has to face about his failure at the Grail Castle, and the second from a woman; it reminds us once more of the nature of the events and of their significance, adding a good number of details, the most important of which is the elaboration of the consequences of Perceval's failure. This is now seen to have repercussions for individuals living in the land of the Fisher King, not simply him alone (4669–83). The description of the widows, lands laid waste, distraught damsels, orphans, and dying knights bears a remarkable resemblance to Perceval's mother's account of the interregnum between Uther and Arthur (435 ff.), but the blame in this case is laid fairly and squarely at the feet of Perceval. Great emphasis is put on Perceval's failure to speak, and more particularly to translate his visual curiosity into words (4653–68). Communication is therefore not only important between people, but also between the different senses of a particular individual.

The vigour of his cousin's reaction to Perceval's admission of silence followed by this second reproach forms the crescendo of Chrétien's orchestration of the theme of word and silence (cf. Ribard, *79*, p.76). The language is once again characterised by words of misfortune ('maleüreus', 4662, 4665; 'mal eür', 4667; 'mal', 4687). Perceval is given no opportunity to reply. The damsel then proposes to the assembled company two adventures which can lead to the acquisition of knightly esteem (4685 ff.). The adventures are graded in order of social usefulness and corresponding honour to be gained. The Château Orgueilleux seems to be a tournament where any knight seeking a joust may find one; the presence of many ladies to witness the deeds confirms the essentially worldly nature of the adventure. The highest worldly esteem, however, ('le pris... / De tot le mont', 4701–02) is to be had at Montesclaire; raising the siege and liberating the damsel will bring not only honour but also the Sword of the Strange Hangings ('l'Espee as Estranges Renges'). Effectively, three adventures are open to the knights: the Château Orgueilleux, Montesclaire, and the Grail. Significantly, Arthur's own knights do not choose to seek the Grail, the distinction between the Grail quest and the others being made quite clear by Perceval's response to the damsel's reproach. He does not protest, but silently accepts his responsibility (4727–40; cf. Frappier, *33*, p.145). Gauvain, the best of Arthur's knights, aims for the highest worldly honour, Girflet will go to the Château Orgueilleux, and Keendin to the Mont Douloureux, this last hitherto unmentioned (4718–26). Whilst for Perceval worldly adventures are a preliminary to the Grail, the other knights regard them as an end in themselves. This is the real importance of the crucial line: 'Et Perchevax redist tout el' (4727) which sets Perceval apart from the others (cf. Frappier, *34*, p.182) and confirms his 'election'. Perceval is now aware of the significance of the Grail adventure and the consequences of his failure, now knows the terms in which the unspelling questions must be put, and seems to know that the Grail Castle cannot be sought as such, but that it will appear to those whose deeds make them worthy of it (cf. Fowler, *32*, p.48).

The stage is therefore set for Perceval to be separated once more from the court and the possibility is opened for Chrétien to follow the adventures of knights other than Perceval. The potential for this was present in *Lancelot*, where the hero and Gauvain both independently set out to seek the abducted Guenièvre, although only Lancelot's adventures were described in any detail (cf. Schmolke-Hasselmann, *87*, p.9). It was necessary for the narrative of that romance that Gauvain failed where Lancelot succeeded, and since Chrétien's concern was largely the relationship between the hero and the queen, it was enough to suggest that Gauvain's lack of love was responsible for his failure. However, since something a good deal more profound and mysterious than love between man and woman seems to be at stake here, and since Perceval alone seems destined to be the hero of the adventure of adventures, Chrétien will try and demonstrate exactly what distinguishes Perceval from the others, in particular the great Gauvain. This will entail a lengthy and detailed series of adventures involving Arthur's nephew. Yet Gauvain will not even set out for Montesclaire to free the damsel and win the sword, for his departure is blocked by an accusation levelled against him by Guigambresil (4759–65). The importance of saving the honour of the lineage takes precedence over the mere acquisition of knightly reputation. Guigambresil's accusation and challenge, as well as Gauvain's response, are all couched in formalistic, even legalistic, terms: Gauvain is not accused of killing Guigambresil's lord, but of having done so without a challenge; he is therefore accused in public of treason (cf. Bloch, *20*, p.37, note 67, and Le Rider, *60*, pp.221 ff.). Gauvain's offer of amends leaves open the possibility that he has behaved wrongly and certainly does not amount to an outright denial (4779–87). His departure is in the same extravagant style as his speech, for he takes seven squires, seven horses and two shields, and leaves to the sound of lamentation from all the ladies of the courts, beating their breasts and tearing

their hair (4804–13). That we are about to leave Perceval and follow
Gauvain is made quite clear by the formula of transition (4814–15).
Gauvain, Arthur's right-hand man, belongs at the court which he is
leaving; his departure therefore suggests a move into the unknown
(cf. Pickens, *73*, pp.34–35).

3. The Adventures of Gauvain

Not all scholars accept that Chrétien intended *Perceval* to be read as I have just suggested, as two sets of adventures commenting on each other. The doubt is caused first of all by the unfinished state of the romance. Secondly, such a structure would be unique in Chrétien's *œuvre*, although the potential for it can be found in earlier works. Thirdly, the so-called hermit episode (6216–58) with Perceval as the central figure occurs apparently unprepared for in the middle of the Gauvain sequence. Finally, the Gauvain adventures are in some respects so different from the rest of Chrétien's work that this has been taken as an indication that they are not by him at all. The divergence of opinion can be gauged by merely noting the positions of the following scholars:

1) Ph.-Aug. Becker (*18*) was of the opinion that Chrétien's part ends at line 3427 with Perceval's visit to the Grail Castle and that the rest is the work of a continuator.

2) Stefan Hofer (*45*) thought that Chrétien was responsible for all the Perceval episodes, including the Good Friday scene (which is therefore displaced); the Gauvain adventures, and the disposition of the extant manuscripts, are due to early scribes and continuators.

3) D.D.R. Owen (*71*), following Gustav Gröber and Ernst Hoepffner, believes that the Perceval and Gauvain parts are separate unfinished romances by Chrétien joined by an early scribe; the hermit episode is an interpolation not written by Chrétien.

4) Leo Pollmann (*76*) does not attribute the Gauvain adventures to Chrétien, but to one of his less gifted disciples; the number of lines attributed to Chrétien is calculated more precisely by stylistic and other means.

Further details can be found in the studies themselves and commentary on the various theories in the studies of Jean Frappier (*36*, *37*, *38*) and David Hoggan (*47*). Adherents to such theories are today in a small minority, since our view of Chrétien's art has changed so significantly over the past few decades that we are now much more inclined to attribute the strangeness of *Perceval* to design rather than accident.

It is true that the Gauvain adventures are in some respects different from the rest of Chrétien's *œuvre*. This has been used either in support of one or more of the theories mentioned above or as evidence that from line 4816 onwards *Perceval* consists of a series of unfinished drafts (cf. Micha, *67*, p.127). Apart from the fact that, to the best of my knowledge, such drafts exist for no other twelfth-century romances, many of the adventures are so lacking in apparent logic that it is difficult to imagine what they could be rough drafts of. Affirmations of the strangeness of the Gauvain adventures are to be found in the work of a number of scholars. Paule Le Rider, for example, has remarked that: 'Tout d'abord à la lecture du *Gauvain*, le lecteur éprouve une sorte de gêne' (*60*, p.211; cf. also p.299). Per Nykrog (*69*) has put this disorienting nature down to Chrétien's precocious modernity and suggests that *Perceval* should be approached in a different way from his other romances. An apparent lack of relevance to the first half of the romance (cf. Owen, *71*, p.154) has also meant that the Gauvain part has been the object of less comment than the adventures of Perceval (cf. Lacy, *59*, p.155). The result is that *Perceval* has not been studied as Chrétien probably conceived it, the fascination of the Grail diverting attention from the work of art as a unity. There have, however, been recent attempts to redress the balance and a growing awareness exists that we have not been doing justice to Chrétien's intentions (cf. Nykrog, *69*, pp.267–68; Le Rider, *60*, p.358; and Ribard, *79*, p.5). The reduced frequency of references to other scholars' work in this chapter reflects their neglect of the Gauvain adventures.

Gauvain seems to have been the earliest and most popular of Arthurian figures, and it looks as if stories concerning him circulated in both the British Isles and France well before Chrétien began to write (cf. Gallais, *40*, and Busby, *23*, pp.30–49). Chrétien, using both written sources such as Wace's *Brut* and oral tales which we no longer possess, gives a place of increasing prominence to

Gauvain in his romances, from a few lines in *Erec et Enide* to half of the extant romance in *Perceval*. In all of the romances Gauvain functions to some degree as a contrast or foil for the hero by virtue of his position as the finest of Arthur's knights. Because of this, Gauvain's 'character' does not undergo any development in the course of a particular poem, although Chrétien's attitude towards him can be seen to change. Michelle A. Freeman goes so far as to suggest that the presentation of Gauvain in *Perceval* is a *bilan* of his appearances in the other romances (*39*, p.133, but cf. Ribard, *80*, p.7). As extensive as his adventures are, Chrétien's Gauvain is not destined to be the hero of romance.

In *Yvain* and *Lancelot*, Chrétien contrasts the heroes, inspired by love for their respective ladies, with Gauvain as a wise, courteous and valiant knight, but one who seems to lack their inspiration. If it was necessary to show Yvain carrying out deeds of chivalry to restore his reputation, it was not necessary to have him do what Gauvain could not; if it was necessary for Gauvain to fail on the quest for Guenièvre, it was not necessary to show him floundering in the river in rusty armour and having to be fished out with boat-hooks (*Lancelot*, *7*, 5125 ff.). Chrétien treats the figure of Gauvain with a certain amount of liberty and an increasing burlesque without at any time suggesting that he is a poor knight or that the values he stands for are fundamentally worthless (although they may be sterile if pursued in a selfish and vainglorious manner). Indeed, it is the contrast between Gauvain and the hero that assures Arthur's nephew of a permanently exalted position, for there would have been little point in comparing a hero with a knight of no standing (cf. Busby, *23*, pp.50–82).

We are therefore justified in the course of the commentary on the Gauvain adventures in drawing comparisons with the Perceval part (cf. Frappier, *33*, p.214). A first observation concerns the original reasons for the departure of the two protagonists. Perceval at the beginning of the romance was a young lad without a past, without a reputation, and without an identity; much of the poem is concerned with his acquisition of these. For Gauvain, however, the problem is quite the opposite: he has a long history, both within the text and without, a reputation second to one, and a name to match (cf. Ribard, *79*, p.109). It is in fact his past that causes him to leave court in an attempt to deal with Guigambresil's accusation, and this same past will confront him on a number of occasions (cf. Kellermann, *52*, p.147).

Gauvain in Tintagel (4816–5655)

There is no description of Gauvain's immediate journey after leaving court, and we find him *en route* as he meets a company of knights. Perceval's mother would have approved of his first questions to the squire, and the wisdom of her advice is proven, since the names of Dröés d'Avés, Meliant de Lis and Tibaut de Tintagel are identical in Gauvain's mind with their reputations. There is a certain resemblance between the story of Meliant de Lis and that of Perceval's brothers, as they, too, were sent by an ailing father to be raised and made knight in another court. The story now related by the squire is a standard one in which a girl requires a young knight to prove himself before granting her love.

In contrast with Perceval, who knew no-one, and for whom everything was new, Gauvain's first encounter outside court is with the familiar world of chivalry, even to the extent of his knowing the persons involved. He is therefore still very much in the Arthurian realm (but cf. Le Rider, *60*, p.246). We have witnessed the granting of a woman's love to a young knight earlier in the romance, but the difference — and it may be significant — is that Perceval had won Blancheflor's love thanks to his selfless and charitable lifting of the siege of Biaurepaire, whereas the motivation for this tournament is on the one hand selfish and on the other epicurean. Indeed, as Haidu has pointed out (*43*, pp.204–05), the beloved's reasons for making Meliant earn her love (that pleasures bought dearly are sweeter than those had with no effort, 4861–63) are similar to the sentiments expressed by Gauvain himself when urging Yvain to leave Laudine in *Yvain* (*5*, 2513–23). There is also a note of irony in the squire's comment about the power love exerts over those it has at its command (4871–74).

What at first seemed an ordinary tournament (not necessarily a serious matter except for purposes of prestige) turns out to have taken a much graver turn in the light of Meliant's intentions (4894–95) and the measures taken to fortify the castle against attack (cf. Le Rider, *60*, pp.243–45). Chrétien stresses the lack of routes open if Gauvain is to make any progress (4910–13) and the fact that the gate is closed (4914). There may here be a double association with some of Perceval's adventures, firstly with his arrival at Biaurepaire (where the gate was closed, 1718–19), and secondly with his inability to avoid the Grail Castle owing to the lack of boat or bridge. The extravagant nature of Gauvain's *équipage* leads the old vavassor to believe that there must be two knights, not one (4932–37). This vavassor has his counterpart in Clamadeu's 'maistre' in the Biaurepaire episode (2393 ff.), for both advise their lords on a particular course of action during a siege. The relationship between the episodes is something like a mirror image: Clamadeu's counsellor on the outside recommends the besiegers to prepare a 'passive' course and effectively to starve the enemy into surrender (2401–27), whereas Tibaut's vavassor on the inside advises the besieged party to take the fight to the opponents (4932–48).

Gauvain is now for a second time taken for what he is not by someone in the tower. This episode is told from the perspective of those in the tower, looking down on Gauvain, who is locked out of the castle, and therefore at a natural disadvantage. The attention alternates between the events of the tournament and speculation about the identity and intentions of the knight below. We are soon involved in a case of 'sibling rivalry' between the two daughters of Tibaut; the elder of the two (who remains nameless) is the beloved of Meliant de Lis and the younger, the Pucelle aux Manches Petites. The initial presentation of the sisters is calculated to establish sympathy for the younger one, especially as Meliant's *amie* has to resort to violence to deal with her sister. Meliant's performance is cause for satisfaction to his beloved, but her repeated evaluation of it provokes her sister's repeated contradictions, and she eventually inflicts physical damage on the little girl (5048–49). The

condemnation of the other ladies present confirms any disapproval
the listener may already have felt (5050–51).

Attention now switches to Gauvain in the meadow, and the
speculations of the ladies are marked by a tone of mischievous
sarcasm. The question has changed from why one knight needs two
shields to why he has not joined in the tournament. The answers
provided range from the acceptable (he is sworn to peace, 5058) to
the positively insulting (he is a horse-dealer, 5062; he is a money-
changer, 5063; he is a profiteer, 5083–85). Such financial activities
were incompatible with the nobility and social status of a knight in
the late twelfth century, and the accusation cuts two ways: either
Gauvain is an *arriviste* horse-dealer pretending to be a knight or a
knight pretending to be a horse-dealer and betraying his profession.
Only the Pucelle aux Manches Petites shares the insight the
audience is privileged to have, that this is no horse-dealer or money-
changer, but a great knight (5079). The whole discussion revolves
around the problems of appearance and reality (5077, 5079, 5082,
5083), and also illustrates Gornemant's advice to Perceval not to
talk too willingly and out of turn. To the Pucelle aux Manches
Petites, the horses and lance have the basic and simple primary
meaning of knighthood. A lack of charity in the others leads to the
distortion of reality and condemnation without a trial. This is the
second time that Gauvain has had to listen to accusations of varying
seriousness, the first charges being those of Guigambresil which led
both to his departure and, indirectly, to his inactivity and the second
accusation.

The narrator expresses his approval of Gauvain's self-restraint
(5095), for the shame that he could bring upon himself and his
lineage by endangering his safety and failing to keep his covenant
with Guigambresil is not worth the risk. Moreover, there may be
implicit criticism of tournament habits, for many participants seem
to regard the occasion as one for making profit by gathering up and
secreting pieces of armour and equipment (5112–13). The misjudg-
ment of both the ladies and the greedy squire is now made apparent,
to the latter's cost. Again, the tone is one of sarcasm, this time
somewhat heavier, not only in the words of the lady in the tower,

but also in those of the squire, addressing a great knight with the pejorative 'Vassax' (5142), and impertinently asking why he has not taken part in the proceedings. Gauvain's tart reply deters the squire from pursuing the matter (5147–53).

The establishing of the vavassor as a sympathetic and credible figure (cf. Foulon, *30*, and Woledge, *94*) enables Chrétien to confirm the approval the narrator had offered (5095) of Gauvain's reasons for not participating (5200–03). The other inhabitants persist in their misappraisal of Gauvain, and the quarrel between the sisters is taken up again (5210 ff.). The elder sister advises her father to take Gauvain prisoner (in order to spite her sibling) and the error spreads a stage further when the father agrees, although he has no more reason than the ladies, the elder sister, or the squire before him, to suspect Gauvain of being anything other than what he seems.

The unpleasant and vindictive nature of the elder sister is tempered first by the sympathy of the vavassor and secondly by the charm and innocent vivaciousness of the Pucelle aux Manches Petites. The relationship of the Pucelle and the daughters of Garin, the vavassor, counterbalances that of her father and Garin, but whereas that between the girls is one of childlike joy (5244–54; cf. also 5467), that of the parents is marked by distrust and conflict. It is only a formally phrased threat to break the feudal bond between lord and vassal (5276–81) that makes Tibaut withdraw his accusation (now a received idea) that Gauvain is a horse-dealer, again in formal terms. Once more, the over-hasty nature of the appraisal of Gauvain is evidenced by Tibaut's approval of his motives for not participating in the tournament (5312–13). There may be a slight hint of approval of trading in Gauvain's assurance that he will survive providing he can find food and lodging that can be bought (5324–30).

It is perhaps an exaggeration to talk in terms of parody (cf., however, Haidu, *43*, pp.210–11), but the relationship between Gauvain and the Pucelle is clearly based on the traditional relationship between knight and damsel whilst at the same time it cannot be taken seriously because of the girl's age. As in romance in general, the ages of the characters in *Perceval* are not specified, but it is clear that the Pucelle aux Manches Petites is too young for the role: she grasps Gauvain's leg to attract his attention (5334–35) and is small enough to be carried off on the neck of her father's horse (5386–87) or in his arms (5429–30, cf. Le Rider, *60*, p.248). Despite this, Gauvain insists on reacting in the traditional way and casts himself as the Pucelle's champion (5379–81). His behaviour can be seen as indulging the whim of a little girl, but given the risk to which he is exposing himself and his mission, we may wonder whether there is not a more serious and critical undercurrent to the delicate whimsy of the episode: despite all that has repeatedly been said about the importance of his meeting with Guigambresil, he will endanger it just to please a pretty nymphet.

The exchanges between Gauvain and the Pucelle are characterised by the vocabulary of courtly love with the formality of the champion-damsel relationship: 'Qu'a vos clamer me sui venue' (5337), 'Qu'a vos de ma seror me claim' (5345), 'Mes enfes dols et debonaire' (5363), '...por amor de moi / Porterez armes au tornoi' (5367–68), 'amie chiere' (5369), and particularly:

> "Sire, se Damediex m'aït,
> Ains a trop bone enfance dite
> Come pucele si petite,
> *Ne ja ne l'en refuserai,*
> *Mais quant li plaist, demain serai*
> *Une piece ses chevaliers.*" (5376–81)

As Frappier has said: 'Gauvain sait tourner de jolies phrases' (*33*, p.222). Gauvain has himself unwittingly been the cause of the dispute between the sisters, although this is not used by the Pucelle in her attempts to persuade him to be her champion. In fact, he accepts the request without enquiring about the cause, attracted by the delicious prospect of being the first knight to fight on her behalf (5369–71; cf. Frappier, *33*, pp.222–23).

Tibaut now enters the spirit after the Pucelle explains to him the origins of the dispute. The Pucelle's explanation also serves as one of the periodic narrative summaries of recent events that we have noted elsewhere. A delightful touch is added in the unsuitability of the Pucelle's sleeves as a token for Gauvain, which requires her father to provide a more appropriate one (5421–28, 5450–60). This is indicative of the nature of the whole episode: the Pucelle is fundamentally unsuited to the role she has assumed, but indulgence by Gauvain and her father lends a playful appearance of suitability to the relationship. This is guaranteed by 'cortoisie' (5417), whereas disapproval of the elder sister's behaviour is expressed by its lack of the same: 'N'avez mie fait que cortoise' (5446).

The rest of the episode restates and expands on motifs and themes launched earlier. Gauvain goes to church before the tournament, and the Pucelle approaches him in the courtliest of ways, except for the childish eagerness apparent in the world 'saut':

> Contre monseignor Gavain saut
> La pucele et dist: "Diex vos salt
> Et doinst honor hui en cest jor.
> Mais portés por la moie amor
> Ceste mance que je tien chi." (5489–93)

We now resume the earlier perspective of looking down on the tournament from the tower in the company of all the women (5499 ff.). The words of the elder sister at the approach of Meliant have a peculiar resonance in the present context, as they repeat almost verbatim lines from the Perceval part of the romance (the words of the fool in lines 1061–62): 'Ainz dist: "Dames, veez venir/Celui qui de chevalerie / A le los et la seignorie"'(5510–12). This will be Gauvain, not Meliant, but only in the immediate context of this episode. The words of the elder sister are therefore doubly inadequate, for their field of application is drastically restricted when compared with the earlier prediction of Perceval's achievement, and even within that restricted field, she is wrong. The defeat of Meliant leads to a further bitter exchange between the sisters as a result of which the elder of the two has to be restrained again from

striking her sister (5539–61). Thematically, we are reminded of
Keu's treatment of the laughing maiden and the fool, both of whom
make truthful predictions which provoke him to violence. In both
cases, the true evaluation of Perceval and Gauvain, neither of whom
seem to be what they are, is expressed by characters who might not
initially be taken as trustworthy (cf. Haidu, *43*, pp.209–10). This is
a good example of the subtle parallelism Chrétien has constructed
between the two major narrative sections of *Perceval*.

Gauvain has clearly been inspired to great deeds in the tournament and the narrator himself expresses, via the squire, his
opinion of Gauvain's mastery (5568–73). The question is whether
inspiration is an appropriate reaction to a playful indulgence of a
little girl's fancy, and more important, whether Gauvain was right
to endanger his mission to Escavalon (cf. Busby, *23*, p.100; see also
Kellermann, *52*, p.149). Certainly, a lack of responsibility is
apparent throughout the episode: flirtatiousness and a desire for
immediate and momentary prestige put at risk a much profounder
type of honour. After defeating Meliant, Gauvain eagerly continues
in the tournament, even though this is not necessary. The game is
played out to the full as the victorious knight sends the horses of his
defeated opponents back, first to the Pucelle aux Manches Petites,
and then to the wife and daughters of his host. Finally, Gauvain
swears eternal service to the Pucelle in the most eloquent and
traditional of terms (5604–10). There is a touch of chivalric
automatism here (and elsewhere) in Gauvain's behaviour: he
responds automatically to the situation, whether the response is
appropriate or not (cf. Le Rider, *60*, p.272). Tibaut de Tintagel,
initially inclined to support the horse-dealer theory, now offers
profuse apologies for his lack of hospitality (5626–34). Again, the
importance of name and reputation is stressed. The Pucelle's final
gesture in kissing Gauvain's foot (5638–40) is touching and irresist-
ible in its comic incongruity, for Gauvain is still on horseback.
Gauvain's parting words are of consummate courtesy and round the
episode off perfectly (5649–52).

Gauvain in Escavalon (5656–6216)

Gauvain's pursuit of the white doe on the edge of a forest is redolent of mythological and literary associations. The white does is traditionally the harbinger of the Other World, bringing the hero into contact with the unknown, and the location of the forest is appropriate as the *locus* of adventure and danger in romance. It may be doubted whether a palfrey (5671) is a suitable horse for hunting deer, and whether a lance is the correct weapon; the pursuit is therefore encumbered by the wrong choice of equipment (cf. Haidu, *43*, pp.212–13). The hunt fails and Gauvain's entry into the Other World is blocked, or at least delayed. Since his horse has lost a shoe, Gauvain, like Perceval, is now looking for a smith (5699–702). The failed hunt is symbolic, for it suggests Gauvain's unsuitability for the role of hero in the Other World, where he will eventually arrive on a lame horse, a condition that has obvious consequences for his effectiveness as a knight (cf. Frappier, *33*, p.225). There is a parallel between the next scene and Perceval's meeting with the Fisher King. Both Perceval and Gauvain are in some discomfiture; the parties they meet are involved in a form of sporting activity, and we focus in both instances first on two persons (3000, 5714), then on one of them (3007 ff., 5715–16). On both occasions, an offer of hospitality follows the meeting, after which Perceval and Gauvain arrive at their host's castle. Roger Dragonetti has pointed out that there is also a parallel between Perceval's hunting in the Gaste Forest during which he encounters the five knights, and Gauvain's hunt of the white doe and his encounter with the party from Escavalon (*28*, p.145). For both, it is an encounter with inhabitants of an unknown world.

The huntsman's instructions to his sister, to be transmitted via the escort, are suggestive of the euphemistic language of courtly love: 'J'ai une seror molt cortoise, / Qui de vos grant joie fera' (5724–25); 'Tel solas et tel compaignie/Li face qui ne li griet mie' (5739–40). If the audience is anticipating an amorous encounter in the light of Gauvain's literary reputation as a womaniser (cf. Haidu,

43, p.214), the narrator's remarks in lines 5748–53 also indicate that complications are to be expected, and moreover that Gauvain has arrived, unawares and on a lame horse, at his destination.

The name Escavalon has undeniable otherworldly associations, and especially after the hunt of the white doe, the audience may have been expecting a land of marvels. The description of the castle, however, could hardly be more mundane, and although there is a touch of splendour about it, the splendour is worldly rather than otherworldly. We have had occasion earlier to remark on Chrétien's apparent approval of trade and mercantile activity, and the same could be read into lines 5758 ff.; all of the objects manufactured are associated either with the profession of knighthood or with the leisure activities and luxurious clothing of the nobility (cf. Frappier, *33*, p.226). The Grail Castle had appeared much more mysterious in comparison. Nor is there anything otherworldly about the relationship that now develops between Gauvain and the sister of the hunter. Gauvain's escort transmits the message as his master had commanded, but once more, the phrasing is somewhat suggestive, and contains a touch of authorial irony: 'Or gardez ne soiez avere/ De tote sa volenté faire, / Mais large et franche et debonaire' (5800–02). The flirting begins as soon as the two are alone, with full co-operation of the girl. The narrator, too, seems to connive in the flirtation (5825–26), looking on as Gauvain swears eternal fidelity. There is certainly nothing very profound about this relationship, and the only thing that is 'courtly' about it is the language in which it is couched. Haidu (*43*, p.215) calls it, and Gauvain's love-affairs in general, 'a formalized social pass-time'.

The interruption of the pair *in flagrante delicto* has already been prepared by lines 5748–50 and more recently by lines 5821–23: 'Et tant estoit bien affaitie/Que pas ne cuide estre agaitie/ De che qu'ele est sole avec lui.' The vavassor recognises Gauvain as the slayer of the girl's father, the King of Escavalon, but his tirade is directed at her rather than at Gauvain, and is full of standard medieval anti-feminist sentiment. The harangue is delivered at the very moment the dramatic irony of Gauvain's situation is revealed to him and confirmed to the audience. The tone is similar to that employed by the Orgueilleux de la Lande talking to Perceval about his *amie* in lines 3855 ff., and both women are innocent of the charges levelled against them. In both cases, the women are accused of sexual motivation, and lines 5864–65 are remarkably similar to lines 3863–64: 'Quant feme puet avoir ses aises,/Del soreplus petit li chaut' (5864–65); 'Feme qui se bouche abandone/Le sorplus molt de legier done' (3863–64). It is, moreover, perverseness that makes a woman a woman. The tirade is marked by a mixture of cynical anti-feminism and a resentful form of hatred towards Gauvain. Unusually in the work of Chrétien, the vavassor here is an unsympathetic figure, encouraging the commons to attack Gauvain, an uncourtly, unchivalric and anarchic course of action.

Even given the stylized conventions of romance, where characters weep and faint and fight hard, long, and often, the piling up of incident upon incident during the siege suggests a particular comic intention on Chrétien's part. The accusation of treason is not new, but it is even more insulting to Gauvain when coming from the mouths of an undisciplined rabble (5916–33). The deliberations of the rabble are characterised by the same mixture of cynical anti-feminism and hatred as that found in the tirade of the vavassor. Everything about the siege is uncourtly, from the 'vilains' with their axes and picks and improvised shields to the horrendous noise they make, not to mention the most unseemly and unladylike language of the girl as she tries in vain to justify her behaviour with Gauvain: 'Hui, hui, fait ele, vilenaille, / Chien esragié, pute servaille!' (5955–56). Technically, her defence is correct: they should not be attacking Gauvain since her brother had taken him under his protection, and, in any case, she is only carrying out her brother's wishes by offering Gauvain 'compaignie, joie et solas' (5972). In an increasing burlesque, Gauvain ('Li portiers', 5989) defends the door single-handed whilst his companion hurls the chess-pieces down on the rabble below, accompanied by more oaths: 'The episode which began in the privacy of the boudoir ends in farcical public shambles' (Haidu, *43*, p.218). Leslie Topsfield sees Gauvain's defence of the tower as a burlesque counterpart of Perceval's defence of

Biaurepaire (*93*, p.274), which would cast further doubt on Gauvain as a hero.

The anarchy of Escavalon is further stressed when the commons refuse to obey Guigambresil's order to desist from the assault (6047–48). In addition, the scrupulous formality of Guigambresil contrasts with the violence and hatred of the vavassor and the mob. The young King of Escavalon underscores this when he returns and discovers Gauvain's identity; although he has harboured his enemy, the rules of courtesy oblige him to protect his guest (6078–80). Nevertheless, the seriousness of the accusation against Gauvain is stressed by the use of the word 'traïson' (6065, 6095, 6106). The quandary that Guigambresil and his king find themselves in is a legal one. The rest of this episode is marked by a sense of legality and formality, as is appropriate, for Gauvain is after all engaged in a quest to prove his innocence of murder and to save the family honour.

The solution suggested by the vavassor requires Gauvain to swear another oath. The oath forms a link between the Perceval and Gauvain parts of the romance, for the vavassor proposes that the combat be postponed for a year to enable Gauvain to go in search of the Bleeding Lance; if he fails to bring it to the king he will place himself once more at his mercy (6110–18). Whilst the proposition at first seems reasonable, the motivation behind it is less than well-intentioned. The implied impossibility of finding the Lance (because it is associated with the Grail, which only Perceval is destined to find) means that Gauvain will have to return to Escavalon where the king will have a legally sounder case against him. The vavassor's advice seems to have been offered out of a desire to harm Gauvain rather than out of a sense of justice. The terms offered directly to Gauvain (6160–67), however, are quite unacceptable since the clause about returning to Escavalon is omitted; failure to find the Lance would cause Gauvain to perjure himself. The original form of the oath is therefore reinstated (6186–91). The narrator suggests (6202–03) that Gauvain is lucky to have escaped this time, but the seriousness of the situation is indicated by Gauvain's dispensing with his entourage and leaving alone. Frappier (*33*, p.230) suggests that Gauvain's quest for the Lance may be a 'quête illusoire' and that for the second time he is a 'quêteur malgré lui', underlining the difference between Gauvain and Perceval, who undertook the second stage of his quest for the Grail of his own free will.

Perceval and his Hermit Uncle (6216–6518)

The unprepared reintroduction of the Bleeding Lance, which once more reinforces the impression that the worlds through which Perceval and Gauvain pass are full of people with unexplained knowledge of the Grail and associated mysteries, paves the way for a momentary *rapprochement* with Perceval's adventures. The wording of the narrative formula in lines 6212–16 not only announces the switch of subject, but also implies the narrator's approval of 'li contes' and complicity between the narrator and the tale. The adventures of Gauvain had been largely devoid of any religious content, but with the return of the narrative to Perceval, we are confronted again with religious concerns related to those that had proven so important in earlier parts of the romance. The reintroduction of the religious element serves, as Erich Köhler has said, to stress that human love is subordinate to divine love, and that its courtly variant may even be a threat to social order (*55*, pp.183–84). When Perceval re-enters the romance, five years have passed since his departure from Arthur's court, at the same moment that Gauvain left for Montescleire. Whilst chronology is rarely exact in Chrétien's works, the time gap, which represents a leap into the future by five years, is disorienting in its suddenness and magnitude (cf. Frappier, *33*, pp.148–49).

Perceval has fulfilled only the first part of the mission he had set himself in lines 4727–40, for the five years of seeking strange and dangerous adventures have not led him back to the Grail Castle. It is implied, although not stated explicitly, that whilst his chivalric performance is excellent, his spiritual state is inadequate, which in turn renders the last five years futile (6220–27; cf. Frappier, *33*, p.149). The five-year failure to go to church and pray stems from a total neglect of one of the pieces of advice offered by both his mother and Gornemant de Gorhaut (592–94; 1663–70), and represents the complete domination of worldly chivalric concerns over spiritual ones, of *militia* over *ecclesia*, of *cupiditas* over *caritas*. His encounter with the penitents on Good Friday provides a pointed contrast with the meeting with the knights at the beginning of the romance. There in the depths of the fertile but uncultivated forest, the place of adventures, the uncultivated 'nice' had first come into contact with chivalry; here in the adventureless desert, a much more experienced and wiser man is forcefully reminded that life consists of more than knightly adventures. There, the crudely dressed peasant lad, astonished by the dazzling beauty of the knights' armour, had learned from the knights some (admittedly superficial) facts about knighthood, before being directed to Arthur's court to learn more; here, the penitents, barefoot and clad in hairshirts (6246), are astonished by the fully-armed Perceval, who is reminded of some basic facts of the Christian doctrine of penitence (cf. Ribard, *78*, p.74). The desert evokes, too, the poor ground of the parable of the sower evoked in the Prologue, for the good ground that was the young Perceval has become hard and infertile (cf. Pickens, *73*, p.255).

The emptiness of Perceval's spirit is also suggested by his obliviousness to time, for whereas the young lad in the forest felt natural joy at the coming of Spring, the seasons have now come and gone five times without his having been aware of it (6220–21). Civilisation, courtesy, chivalry are, in this respect at least, seen as repressing rather than stimulating human development. The doctrinal content of the episode is hardly remarkable, but it does not need to be, for all that has to be established is that Perceval is not in a state of grace and that he needs to repent. The repeated emphasis on 'pechiez', this time unambiguously in the sense of 'sin' (6252, 6268, 6271, 6274, 6310), raises once more the question of the nature of Perceval's own fault in not responding to his mother's faint or the suffering of the Fisher King. The explanation of the penitent shocks Perceval out of his state of inertia into a desire to confess; the visit to the hermit will provide the second and stronger stage of the shock, leading to the final realisation of his error (cf. Frappier, *33*, p.153 and Kellermann, *52*, pp.113 ff.).

The desert is both a place of infertility and a place of holiness, traditionally the dwelling-place of saints. The hermit in *Perceval* resides in a wood at the edge of the desert, and it is through this wood that Perceval now makes his way. In a return to his home environment, the wood, Perceval becomes once more the simple innocent he was before (6351) and embraces the hermit's foot in a childlike gesture (6351, reminiscent of the Pucelle aux Manches Petites and Gauvain?) before beginning his confession. Perceval's confession is used as a means of summarising events at the Grail Castle (6372–86). This is the third reminder of those events and altogether a calmer one, lacking the breathless staccato of Perceval's interrogation by his cousin or the resentful accusations of the Hideous Damsel. Yet if it lacks the tension of the two previous occasions, it is no less profound, and the situation provides an opportunity for remedial action via repentance that the other two did not. Rupert T. Pickens has written of figures such as Perceval's mother, his cousin, his uncle, and the Hideous Damsel, that they 'comprehend dimensions of reality far beyond the immediate and the material' and that it is their task to communicate some of their knowledge to Perceval (*73*, p.252). More important, it now becomes clear that Perceval is related not only to the hermit, but also to the Fisher King and the mysterious king in the side chamber (6415–19). As Daniel Poirion has remarked: 'La famille maternelle semble se resserrer autour du héros' (*74*, p.193). Perceval is descended through his mother from the family of Grail Kings and is the only male on either side of the family to have avoided death or crippling injury. Detailed family trees can be sketched for *Perceval* and other Grail romances, and are given, for example, by Köhler (*55*, p.213) and Schmid (*86*, pp.35–77). Given his uncle's position as a hermit, Perceval would seem to be the only hope of furthering the lineage.

The hermit's 'explanation' of Perceval's sin and gloss on the events at the Grail Castle do not explain very much at all, adding only a few details to what we already know or rendering explicit that which until now has been implicit. The hermit's commentary is prompted by Perceval's revelation of his name (which provoked a somewhat more violent reaction from his sorrowing cousin). The hermit is wrong when he says that Perceval knows nothing of his sin (although *sez* in line 6393 may mean 'comprehend'), since he has already been informed of it by his cousin (3593–95); *pechié*, of course, can mean 'misfortune' as well as 'sin'. According to D.G. Hoggan, Perceval's sin is in confessional terms *voluntarium in causa positiva* in leaving his mother, but *negativa* in that he did not turn back when he saw her faint (*47*); his culpability is nevertheless difficult to ascertain in absolute terms. Perceval now leárns that the Grail serves the father of the Fisher King and brother of the hermit, his uncle. The sustenance derived by the old king from the Host in the Grail recalls the penitent's description of the hermit, his brother: 'Ne ne vit, tant par est sains hom, / Se de la gloire de Dieu non' (6305–06). I take this similarity to be intentional; the Grail would then be the dispenser of God's grace.

The rest of the hermit's advice repeats much of that which Perceval received earlier. New, however, is the advice to honour priests (6461–64), and indeed, there is a very 'priestly' tone to the whole passage which is absent in earlier parts of the romance. The celebration of mass, the hermit's role of confessor and commentator, the associations of the Grail with the mass, and the emphasis placed on the state of Perceval's soul, all contribute to this tone. This episode is a spiritual counterpart to Perceval's visit to Gornemant de Gorhaut, and therefore also a variant of the hospitality sequence so common in romance. Here, instead of the traditional merrymaking of such a sojourn, is the hermit's meagre and meatless fare (6499–504). At the end of the episode, Perceval takes communion, and is in a fit state once more to look for the Grail and ask the questions. As much as a comment on the character of Perceval, the hermit's words constitute a clerical justification of knighthood based on charity and humility (cf. Haidu, *43*, pp.229–30). A formula of transition leads us back to the adventures of Gauvain (6514–18).

None of the theories that cast doubt on the authenticity of the hermit episode or its location have won general acceptance. I have tried to show that, on the contrary, it has strong thematic links to earlier parts of the poem, that it is prepared for by the reintroduction of the Bleeding Lance into Gauvain's Escavalon adventure, and that it serves to remind the audience that this is a romance about the Grail. This kind of alternation of protagonists is not common in Chrétien's works, but there is no reason, stylistic, thematic or otherwise, to indicate that it is anything other than a new artistic departure. The manuscript evidence is also against the interpolation theory, for all extant copies of the romance have the episode in the same place. The episode serves to remind us of the importance of charity in the widest sense of the word, and to cause us to reflect on the meaning of the Gauvain adventures which enclose this momentary return to Perceval. Perceval has seen the insufficiencies of five years of seeking worldly adventures without a spiritual dimension. Chrétien may be trying to tell us that Gauvain's activities are equally barren and lacking in charity.

Greoreas, Galvoie, and the Orgueilleuse de Logres (6519–7370)

The return of the narrative to Gauvain reverses the chronological disturbance of the hermit episode and takes us back five years. As Perceval had done on a number of occasion, Gauvain now encounters a sorrowing damsel sitting beneath a tree (cf. Saly, *85*, pp.23–24), but not before he has remarked on the unusual combination of shield, lance and palfrey (6531–34). Had it been another kind of horse, more suitable for a knight, he would have found it less odd. We are reminded both of the remarks of the ladies in the tower at Tintagel (5052 ff.) and of Gauvain's own inappropriate pursuit of the white doe which led him towards Escavalon (5656 ff.). Like the tent maiden Perceval finds being punished by the Orgueilleux de la Lande, the damsel sorrowing here over a knight would have been beautiful if she had been joyful rather than distressed. Given the injured state of the knight, Gauvain's insistence on waking him up may seem lacking in charity, despite the courteous language in which it is couched (esp. lines 6567–68). When Gauvain does wake the knight by jogging his spur with the blunt end of his lance, the narrator is careful to stress that it was done so gently that no harm could come of it (6584–87). Gauvain's lack of consideration is met, ironically by gratitude (6589–92; cf. Haidu, *43*, pp.234–35).

The theme of 'the land from which no-one returns' is common in romance and had been treated by Chrétien himself in *Lancelot*; it is usually associated with the passage to the Other World (cf. esp. Haug, *44*). The effect of the warning not to proceed is guaranteed to harden the knight's resolve, and Gauvain's sense of honour requires him to persist (6615–23). His insistence on continuing results from a fear of being accused of 'recreandise' (6619) and is, as Le Rider has pointed out, 'sans but' (*60*, p.262). The 'bosne de Galvoie' (6602) is the second in a series of frontiers and borders that Gauvain has to cross (the first having been the passage to Escavalon). The injured knight realises what Gauvain's motivation is and is resigned to the futility of the warning (6624–27); the episode almost becomes a self-conscious literary motif, with the characters behaving as they know the audience would expect them to. Gauvain's promise to return by the same route to check on the knight and the maiden guarantees that he will have to retrace his steps (6651–56). Gauvain then prepares to enter what is an Other World within an Other World. If Galvoie is meant to evoke Galloway in the south-east of Scotland, it may suggest a return to his origins for Gauvain, since in addition to the phonological similarity between the names, an ancient tradition makes Gauvain and his family natives of that area. For Jacques Ribard, this return to his origins symbolises the beginning of Gauvain's attempts to rid himself of the accumulated attributes of a life of worldly knighthood, in preparation for a new formation that would parallel that of Perceval (*80*, p.10).

Despite the unexceptional description of the castle and town to which Gauvain now comes, the maiden he finds in a meadow seated under an elm tree, looking at herself in a mirror, certainly evokes supernatural, possibly diabolic, associations (6659–81; cf. Le Rider, *60*, pp.274–75). However, she is not supernatural, and her beauty belies the aggressiveness with which she addresses Gauvain at his approach (6684 ff.). The first exchange between the two is odd, to say the least. Her warning to Gauvain to exercise moderation and not to waste his time and effort (on what?) elicits a courteous enquiry as to the reason for the warning (6692–95). That she is able to predict Gauvain's intentions suggests either an ability to read minds on her part or a lack of subtlety on his, although the remarkable thing is rather that Gauvain happily admits to the correctness of her guess. Lines 6702 ff. constitute a kind of anti-feminist outburst, yet directed at Gauvain and implicating both sexes, ridiculing a custom. 'Ces foles bretes' (6706) sound like 'those women in romances', and the maiden makes it quite clear to Gauvain that she will not be behaving in the manner which he (and the audience) may be expecting. Gauvain's persistent tolerance of her aggression establishes a distorted version of the traditional relationship between lover and courtly lady common elsewhere (cf. Busby, *23*, pp.109 ff.). Lines 6713–19 sound like a curse, and the use of the word 'vassax' (6723) as a means of address certainly indicates here, as elsewhere, a lack of respect. The world in which Gauvain finds himself is not the one to which he is accustomed, and the unpredictable reactions of characters in familiar situations are unsettling (cf. Lacy, *59*, p.161).

Gauvain is now required to cross a third barrier, namely a plank (6727) that spans an unspecified space over into the garden where the maiden's palfrey is to be found. The narrowness of the plank not only causes Gauvain a practical problem, but also creates a sense of insecurity in that he must abandon Gringalet and go on foot, thereby casting aside for a while his identity as a knight (cf. Busby, *23*, p.110). The spectators' dire predictions of Gauvain's lot, especially the use of the words 'mal' (6753, 6754, 6760, 6765) and derivatives of 'avenir' (6754, 6760, 6766) produce an effect of inevitable misfortune. His reaction to the predictions is somewhat peculiar, for he behaves like modern visiting royalty, greeting the crowds and receiving their greetings in return (6673–75). His self-assurance is disturbingly at odds with the menace of the episode. As Gauvain goes to take the palfrey, he is warned by a knight (like the maiden, sitting under a tree) of the consequences of his act. What at first sight seems a standard pattern which would require the knight himself to challenge and fight Gauvain becomes something different when the challenge turns out to be advice rather than a threat. The knight even specifically says that it is *not* his intention to prevent Gauvain from taking the horse (6788–90). The repeated warnings of doom and decapitation, first from the injured knight (6598 ff.) and then from the crowds and the knight in the garden (6572 ff.; 6802 ff.), together with Gauvain's repeated determination to avoid *recreantise*, create a suspense that is repeatedly deflated.

The palfrey itself, one side of its head white and the other black (6822–23), is a conventional indication of otherworldliness, but the horse has nothing supernatural about it, once again disappointing the expectation aroused. Despite her fairy-like pose, the maiden's admonitions to Gauvain not to touch her and repeated predictions of misfortune are suggestive of an unbalanced mind rather than anything else. Frappier has suggested that the traumatic experience she suffered earlier, revealed later in the romance, has turned her into a '*vamp*' (*33*, p.236, cf. also Holmes and Klenke, *48*, p.64). The assigning of tasks to knights by damsels is, of course, a standard device, and the haughty maiden's initial refusal to grant the knight her love is again conventional, yet there is something profoundly disturbing about the venom of this woman's remarks to Gauvain (cf. Busby, *23*, pp.111–12). The formal courtly relationship is here again weirdly perverted, for the mere offer to help her mount hardly constitutes sufficient grounds for her outburst. The curse of lines 6713–14 is repeated in lines 6862–68, and Gauvain's response is as courteous and placid as the first time; his attempt to offer her her cloak is also met by a torrent of abuse. Her resistance stands in shocking contrast to the apparent alacrity with which the sister of the King of Escavalon accepted Gauvain's advances (5827–31). In neither case, however, is there any question of love, and the implicit comparison between Gauvain's contacts with women and Perceval's is once more telling. All of Gauvain's relationships with women are characterised by some form of inappropriateness in a courtly romance context. Chrétien has also been withholding the names of his protagonists again, for the audience has been told neither that of the injured knight nor that of the damsel (cf. Poirion, *74*, p.193).

For the sake of convenience, however, I shall refer to them by the names Chrétien eventually gives them, Greoreas and the Orgueilleuse de Logres.

Gauvain begins to retrace his steps, for he now returns to the damsel and the wounded knight (6904–09). His recent itinerary may be sketched as follows: Greoreas — Bosne de Galvoie — Orgueilleuse — Plank — Palfrey — Plank — Orgueilleuse — Bosne de Galvoie — Greoreas. His progress has therefore been nil (cf. Busby, *24*). Gauvain's medical knowledge is unexplained here (6910–14), but it does occur elsewhere in Arthurian literature and may refer to a now lost tradition of Gauvain stories (cf. Busby, *23*, p.112 and note 50). There is no initial reason for suspecting that the wounded knight's desire for confession stems from anything other than concern for his soul, but the appearance of the red-haired squire (6985 ff.) indicates trouble. His portrait is grotesque and parodic, and achieves its effect in much the same way as that of the Hideous Damsel, by inverting and subverting the rhetoric of the conventional portrait. Gauvain's attempt to give the squire's nag to the wounded knight leads to what can best (anachronistically) be described as slapstick. Haidu (*43*, pp.235–36) calls the scene 'pure farce' and compares it to early Chaplin. The squire's use of the word 'Vassal' (7014, 7030) and his offensive attitude smack of the Orgueilleuse and hint at a conspiracy, a conspiracy, moreover, of which the wounded knight may even be aware (7007–09). It should be noted that there is a good deal of fisticuffs in *Perceval*, and Chrétien may have intended this scene to remind the audience of Keu's striking the damsel and the fool (1048–57), or of the elder sister's behaviour toward the Pucelle aux Manches Petites (5048–49). It is more likely to be the earlier of the two episodes that is evoked here, especially in the light of the squire's prediction in lines 7036–40, reminiscent of the fool's words to Keu in lines 1260–74.

The narrative possibilities of the theft of Gauvain's horse, Gringalet, and of earlier scenes are created by mistaken identities and the taking of people for what they are not. This theme runs through both parts of *Perceval*, and forms part of what Rupert

74 *Perceval (Le Conte du Graal)*

Pickens sees as a basic structuring device of the romance: 'The *Conte del Graal* is a poem largely "about" signs and the interpretation of signs' (*72*, p.138). After having his identity as a knight endangered by having to ride a lame horse, Gauvain now loses it completely for a while and is humiliated by having to ride the squire's nag (7158 ff.). The theme of inappropriate behaviour noted earlier (of the Orgueilleuse towards Gauvain) is repeated as Gauvain's charitable deed is rewarded by gleeful taunting and expression of hatred (7178–99). The difference here, however, is that the hatred is motivated and explicable in terms of Gauvain's past. As with the Escavalon episode, there is a certain legality about the present scene: Gauvain claims not to be aware of having offended Greoreas (7106–08), but does not exclude the possibility; the charge is made explicit, but Gauvain's guilt or innocence revolves around a legal nicety (7118–40). Greoreas does not seem to object to the punishment *per se* nor does he deny having committed the rape. What he objects to is the fact that Gauvain took the law into his own hands rather than let Arthur judge and sentence him (cf. Le Rider, *60*, pp.290–91). The punishment, procedurally correct or not, fitted the crime in that the rapist loses his reason during the act of rape; it is therefore appropriate that he be forced to eat with dogs. Greoreas's retaliatory deed of stealing Gringalet also hits Gauvain where it hurts.

When Greoreas leaves Gauvain, the taunting is taken over again by the Orgueilleuse in a renewed assault (7147–57, 7178–99). The tone has changed from evil rancour to glee at his plight. The description of the nag reminds us of that of the mount of the tent maiden (3691–714); the humour of both descriptions lies not only in their grotesqueness but also in the way they remind us of the conventions of the human, particularly female, portrait. They refer to a universal romance tradition and specifically to a procedure established within *Perceval* itself (cf. also Kellermann, *52*, p.130). The statements the Orgueilleuse makes are all palpably untrue: Gauvain is not well mounted; he does not look like a knight fit to escort a maiden; the horse is not strong and fit. Gauvain's attempts to chastise her are met with a tart command to shut up (7209).

Struggling pitifully on the nag, Gauvain now comes to a third barrier, a river in front of a splendid castle. In contrast with the other places Gauvain comes to, there is certainly an aura of the supernatural about this one, and Frappier has aptly remarked: 'Quelle vision de mystère et de beauté Chrétien a su imposer ici à l'imagination de ses lecteurs!' (*33*, p.238) Here is an ideal place for a knight to perform great deeds, witnessed by five hundred women (7423–25); more accurately, it is five hundred and one, for the narrator does not allow us to forget that Gauvain is still in the company of 'la plus male rien del mont' (7258). The Orgueilleuse's urging Gauvain to hurry into the boat before he is attacked by the pursuer works in the same way as warnings about the land from which no-one returns and encourages him to stay and fight. It is also possible to see here a commentary on the knight's quest of prowess for its own sake (Le Rider, *60*, p.272). The need to demonstrate his courage is reinforced by the prospect of regaining Gringalet. Again, the Orgueilleuse mysteriously knows who the horse-thief is and what he wants (7301–08). The conspiratorial nature of this part of the romance is also suggested by her assertions that Greoreas's nephew, the pursuer, is intent on causing Gauvain 'male aventure' (7300) and taking his head back to Greoreas. These recall the predictions she has herself made to Gauvain on a number of occasions. If Gauvain had earlier been a knight fit to escort a damsel (7188–89), he is now, according to the Orgueilleuse, fit to joust with another (7324–25) and in front of all the women of the castle, who have come especially for Gauvain (7321). Her words, as usual, are intended ironically, but Gauvain will indeed succeed in impressing the women and in regaining his horse and dignity as a knight. There is a rapidity in the changes of fortune and mood of the Gauvain part of *Perceval* which continuously disorients both reader and protagonist (cf. Busby, *23*, p.117).

The Castle of Marvels (7371–8371)

The idea of the custom has been well discussed by Erich Köhler (*61*), and it will be sufficient here to note that the origins of customs are rarely explained and that they seem to have existed since time immemorial, that some form of violence is usually involved, and that contravention is regarded as undesirable. Acceding to the ferryman's demand (7376–80, 7388–92) and fulfilling the present custom, however, would require surrendering Gringalet once more. From the moment he crossed into Escavalon, Gauvain has had trouble with his horses, his mobility, and his identity as a knight; together with the curses of the Orgueilleuse, this has amounted to his being constantly dogged in his movements and constantly attacked verbally and physically wherever he goes. The ferryman's predictions about the difficulty Gauvain will have capturing the knight (7412–14) prove to be inaccurate as the latter is so badly wounded that he surrenders without a fight. This, too, rejoins the pattern of the earlier episode of the Orgueilleuse's palfrey, for there the expected opposition to retrieving the horse also failed to materialise. Chrétien is thus constantly raising expectations by conventional signs, only to disappoint them and disorient the audience. Whilst he did this to some extent in the Perceval part, it has become the rule since Gauvain's entry into Escavalon.

Gauvain is penetrating more and more deeply into a world in which he is unable to function as efficiently as he did in Arthur's realm. He is also confronted, like Perceval, by characters who seem to know what is going on whilst he himself is quite unaware of it. This is true of the ferryman, who confirms that Gauvain is the latest in a series of knights to become involved with the Orgueilleuse (7453–58). The way in which the ferryman's offer of hospitality is phrased, stressing the danger of the country (7462–65), might lead the audience to think that Chrétien is about to show Gauvain once more refusing to take the advice and stay to preserve his honour; if so, the expectation remains unfulfilled as Gauvain accepts the offer without further ado. What is more unexpected, perhaps, is the luxury in which the ferryman lives and the lavish hospitality he affords Gauvain (7473–93). One function of hospitality sequences, as we have noticed elsewhere, is to provide the hero with information about the situation he is in. The ferryman is paradoxically unable to answer Gauvain's question as to the identity of the lord of the castle, but goes on to explain about the defences and the queen who lives there (7520 ff.).

The river in front of the castle and the ferryman himself may well be intended to evoke the frontier of the kingdom of the dead, and other indications in the text may confirm this (cf. Le Rider, *60*, p.263; Spensley, *89*, p.33; Topsfield, *93*, p.272). Yet Chrétien is not here presenting an unambiguous Other World or realm of the dead, for it is precisely the combination of realism and the supernatural that gives this episode its evocative power. In terms of the overall structure of the romance, it may be a counterpart of the Grail episode (cf. Kellermann, *52*, p.217; Haidu, *43*, pp.243–44).

There is also a parallel between the ferryman's story of the queen's retiring to the castle with her treasure, daughter and grand-daughter and that of the withdrawal to the Gaste Forest of Perceval's parents and their children (407 ff.), a parallel which contributes like many others to the cohesiveness of the romance as a whole. Dragonetti (*28*, p.169) also sees the two queens as counterparts to the two kings of the Grail castle. It is this kind of cohesiveness that makes the structural relationship between the two main parts of *Perceval* so complex. The supernatural character of the castle, suggested by Gauvain's first sight of it, and further hinted at by the description of the defences, is now confirmed by the ferryman. From the latter's words (7582–604), associations with the Saviour and the Harrowing of Hell are unmistakeable, although, as Spensley has pointed out (*89*, p.32), the inhabitants do seem to be there of their own accord. Gauvain determines to visit the palace, and the ferryman's resignation (7627–29) recalls that of Greoreas as Gauvain was about to cross the Bosne de Galvoie (6624–27).

The mysterious atmosphere of the place is sustained as Gauvain meets the 'escacier' (7651). This brief scene is typical of Chrétien's art of creating suspense. He presents something mysterious without explaining any possible significance, and even the ferryman's remarks that the 'escacier' is rich and that Gauvain would have been in danger had it not been for his company (7669–75) are not very enlightening. Frappier has commented on Chrétien's art of mystification in connection with the Grail scene, but the remark is equally applicable here: 'Mais Chrétien n'a-t-il pas compris aussi que son sujet, pour être plus beau, devait rester à demi mystérieux, qu'il n'avait pas à imposer une interprétation trop nette ... mais à proposer seulement des sens probables ou possibles?' (*34*, p.174). The description of the palace (7676 ff.) is a set-piece, but which may suggest a little more than worldly wealth. The bed in particular assumes a place of prominence which may indicate that it will play a role of some importance in the story. Yet despite the scale and lavishness of the palace, there is little hard evidence of the supernatural, and Gauvain sees nothing to support the ferryman's warnings. Again, resignation is the latter's reaction to Gauvain's repeated determination (7812–16). This pattern of warning, determination and resignation has now been repeated four times in this section of the narrative, and combined with the constant predictions of misfortune, produces an unrelieved atmosphere of unease and tension.

What Gauvain saw to be a wonderfully rich bed fit for a nobleman like himself is revealed by the ferryman as 'li Lis de la Merveille' (7805), a bed of death, for no-one has ever sat on it yet and lived. By his success on the bed, Gauvain has managed to free the castle of the enchantments upon it and is now fêted by the inhabitants as a saviour. He has thus satisfied the conditions mentioned by the ferryman in his earlier explanation of the castle and of the folly of awaiting a messiah (7520 ff.). The episode has a number of associations, especially that of Christ's descent into Hell, and within Chrétien's own work, the rescue of Guenièvre and the liberation of the prisoners in *Lancelot* (*7*, 2312 ff.). Comparison is also invited between this visit to the Castle of Marvels and Perceval's to the Grail Castle. Whereas Perceval fails to ask the questions, heal the Fisher King, and restore the land to prosperity, Gauvain passes the test, frees the inhabitants, and becomes lord of the castle. It has also been argued that passing the test exculpates Gauvain from the accusations of Guigambresil, as he has been shown to be free of all vice and sin (cf. Le Rider, *60*, pp.286–87, and Busby, *23*, pp.121–22). Yet it is still not clear whom he has liberated from what, for no more details are forthcoming about the inhabitants or the nature of the enchantments.

Once more, Gauvain has performed great deeds in front of an audience of women, as the Orgueilleuse and ferryman had both suggested he would (7314–14; 7782–86). The welcome he now receives from the women of the castle is all Gauvain could have hoped for. The scene is a combination of conventional hospitality themes and elements specifically appropriate to the present context. Despite the conventional nature of certain aspects of the episode, there is a kind of elaborateness about it that suggests that Chrétien is being purposefully excessive. Gauvain surrounded by his bevy of women, the long and arguably unnecessary explanation of why he should put on the ermine cloak the queen has sent him (7951–68), Gauvain's own hypercourteous reply to the messenger (7971–81; cf. his approach to Perceval in lines 4432–41, and Haidu's analysis of his language, *43*, esp. pp.192 ff.), all seem at the same time familiar but overdone to the extent that the extreme formality masks any significance the events may have. In other words, the rhetoric constitutes the fabric of the scene, and the net effect is one of showiness.

Nevertheless, it does seem as if Gauvain's tribulations are at an end: Guigambresil, the Orgueilleuse, Greoreas, all are forgotten in the sweetness of success. The revelation of the consequences of his success, however, proves to be a sting in the tail. The saviour becomes a prisoner, for he may not leave the castle (8012–24): 'royauté charmante et dérisoire', as Frappier has put it (*33*, p.244). This causes a radical change of mood in Gauvain, who now returns to the bed and sulks (8035–37), another of the touches of psychological realism detected by Kellermann (*52*, p.127). What had seemed to be a lightening of the atmosphere from despair to joy proves to be only a momentary raising of false hope. Gauvain's refusal to eat until he hears better news reminds us of Arthur's traditional pensive state and refusal to eat until an adventure occurs or news is brought to court (cf. Schmolke-Hasselmann, *87*, pp.35 ff.). After the brief greeting, the elder queen's first questions are about Arthur's household and the sons of King Lot (8118 ff.).

Rather than being intended to elicit information she does not
possess, the questions she poses check on Gauvain's knowledge,
confirm her own, and comfort her by the mention of familiar names.
As Gauvain has not actually revealed his identity (since she, oddly
perhaps, did not ask him who he was), he is an anonymous
informant talking about himself, his family and acquaintances to
someone for whom they seem to belong to a familiar kind of past
from which she is somehow cut off. The progressive revelation of
identities noted elsewhere in the romance has its consequences here,
too.

The meal is also a first for Gauvain, as no-one has ever yet
eaten sitting on the Lit de la Merveille (8228–29). Gauvain is once
more surrounded by women looking after his every wish, even to the
extent of placing a pillow under his head at bedtime. The two
hundred and fifty maidens are joined by a number of 'vallets' of
various ages, from young to old and hoary-headed (8236–41). These
are the men who have awaited the arrival of the saviour in order to
be made knights (7563 ff.), but there seems to be something peculiar
about the ageing process in the castle, for 'vallets' elsewhere in
Chrétien's work and outside are without exception young. The
enchantments of the castle therefore have something to do with time
and may relate to the queen's remark about King Arthur being a
100-year-old child (8168–71). Whilst time in romance is rarely, if
ever, chronologically consistent, and indeed contributes to the
general sense of mystery that pervades the genre, the insistence on
the ages of first Arthur and then the 'vallets', not to mention the
three generations of royal women, suggests not so much that time is
important, but that it has been seriously disturbed (cf. Ribard, 79,
p.105).

From high in the tower, Gauvain espies the Orgueilleuse de
Logres and her knight down below (8286–90). After the apparent
isolation in the Castle of Marvels, the narrative edges back towards
the earlier adventure, although, significantly, the distance between
the castle and world outside is symbolised by the perspective. Once
more, characters Gauvain encounters seem to know things he does
not, and it looks more and more as if he is an outsider moving with-

out direction through a world in which all places and persons are interrelated, all events carefully planned (cf. Lacy, *59*, p.160). Gauvain's outraged reaction at being reminded that he is a prisoner and the ferryman's intervention persuade the queen to let him leave, but only on condition that he promises to return by nightfall, *if God defend him from death* (8346). We are reminded of his promise to return to Escavalon, after seeking the Bleeding Lance (6183 ff.). Gauvain's request to the queen not to ask him his name for a week (8350–53) prolongs his incognito, and restates the importance of the theme of name and identity. By recrossing the river in front of the castle, he has retraced his steps once again to rejoin the Orgueilleuse.

Guiromelant and the Reprise of the Orgueilleuse (8372–9234)

The knight accompanying the Orgueilleuse is the one Greoreas had referred to (6609–12) in his warning to Gauvain. Despite Gauvain's victory, the Orgueilleuse does not seem to have changed her attitude towards him, claiming that he was able to defeat her companion only because the latter was injured (8421–33; cf. Keu's words to Gauvain about defeating knights when they are already tired, 4377–80). Nevertheless, she offers Gauvain the chance to put an end to her hostility by leaping over the Gué Périlleux (as her *ami* had done whenever she had wanted him to). The chorus of women witnessing events from the castle restates the theme of the land whence no-one returns (8453–60). Gauvain's resolve to jump over the Gué is hardened by what he has heard about it, namely that the knight who succeeds in the test will gain 'tot le pris del monde' (8510). This had also been said of other adventures earlier (for example, of Montesclaire in lines 4701–14), but the question arises, if Gauvain is in the other world, or even the realm of the dead, of where exactly his fame will spread (cf. Le Rider, *60*, p.263). His achievement in leaping over is diminished by the fact that he is only able to reach the other side after first falling into the water (8511–20). The dependence of Gauvain on his horse is clear again, and the episode not without a touch of parody (cf. Frappier, *33*, p.247).

The network of relationships between the characters Gauvain meets is expanded when the knight he encounters on the other bank claims to have been in love with the Orgueilleuse. Gauvain's successful leap over the Gué is another achievement, for the Orgueilleuse was lying to him when she said that her *ami* had crossed it whenever she wanted (8437–39). The covenant Gauvain now enters into with the knight, to exchange information and knowledge freely, will guarantee during their ensuing conversation revelation and explanation of some of the more mysterious features of recent events, this in contrast with many scenes in the romance where no questions are asked at all.

Gauvain's initial questions (8618 ff.) establish the identity of his new acquaintance (Guiromelant of Orqueneseles, of whom he seems to have heard), his ill-tempered companion (the Orgueilleuse de Nogres) and of her *ami* (the Orgueilleux du Passage à l'Etroite Voie). The scoffing and incredulous tone of Guiromelant's reaction to Gauvain's tale of sitting on the Marvellous Bed (8674–96) recalls the 'ramprosnes' of the ladies in the tower at Tintagel (5054 ff.). Here, too, the point is that Gauvain is said, albeit mockingly, not to be a knight, but to belong to a profession that is accorded a good deal less respect by Guiromelant. In the Tintagel episode, he had been seen as a horse-dealer or money-changer, now he is ignominiously said to be a *jongleur*, so fanciful and fantastic are the lies he tells. The irony is that it is precisely the fantastic and unlikely details of his story, rounded off with a flourish as he shows Guiromelant the lion's claws in his shield (8712), that convince Guiromelant that he is telling the truth.

This conversation may be compared to Perceval's with his cousin (3422 ff.). In both, the protagonist describes to a sceptical listener the events of the previous evening, and in both the protagonist admits to not having asked a question (8727–31). On the first occasion, however, Perceval is reproached with failure, whilst on the second Gauvain is congratulated on his success. In both episodes, the interlocutor informs the protagonist about the significance of some of the events, and in both, it transpires that the protagonist was unbeknown to himself in the company of members of his family (cf. Kellermann, *52*, p.20; Hofer, *45*, p.22; Haidu, *43*, p.247). The story of Ygerne's retiring to the Castle of Marvels is couched in terms similar to those used by Perceval's mother describing her own retreat (442 ff.) and those of the ferryman in his own description of the Castle of Marvels (7572 ff.). The reference to the death of Uther Pendragon (8740–41) situates the retreat of both Perceval's and Gauvain's families in the same period (cf. Delbouille, *26*, p.84).

Gauvain's incognito encounters with both enemies and family can be seen both as a motif and a narrative device in *Perceval*. In the previous scene, Gauvain had guaranteed his anonymity by making the queen promise not to ask his name for seven days; here, his self-imposed custom of always revealing his name when asked brings the enmity out into the open. The proposed battle sets the stage for another sequence of the narrative. Guiromelant's hatred of Gauvain is expressed by dire threats of decapitation and dismemberment comparable to the attitude he encountered in Guigambresil and Greoreas. Here he is involved in a family feud, as his father is supposed to have killed Guiromelant's and he himself one of Guiromelant's cousins (8778–85). The cumulative impression of bloodshed created in the course of the romance is disturbing, and Gauvain does not entirely disprove the various accusations levelled against him (cf. Busby, *23*, p.136, and Le Rider, *60*, p.343, who actually considers Gauvain 'coupable d'homicide'). This kind of killing is inherent in the nature of chivalric society, and the theme may form part of Chrétien's social comment, specifically on the inter-baronial conflict of the times and its vendettas. To complicate matters, Guiromelant is in love with Gauvain's sister, Clarissant. An immediate combat is avoided only because Guiromelant is unarmed and proposes instead to meet Gauvain in seven days' time in front of witnesses from both parties (8845 ff.), underlining the formalistic nature of confrontation noted before in the romance. Being seen to do things properly is paramount as is the increase in honour gained when something is done in public. When Gauvain seems to prevaricate, offering to make amends if he has indeed caused Guiromelant any trouble (8871–78), we are reminded of his reaction to Guigambresil's accusation earlier in the romance (4779 ff.). Leaping unaided back across the Gué, Gauvain has retraced his steps once more (8914–16).

There no longer seems to be any purpose to the adventures of Gauvain, the aim of finding the Bleeding Lance having been lost from view long since (cf. Köhler, *55*, p.249, and Frappier, *33*, p.231). Encounter follows encounter, each precluding him from finishing tasks he has undertaken, everything taking place in a world full of his enemies where he is the only one unaware of what is happening. The encounters coincide with a succession of obstacles (rivers, frontiers, fords, etc.) that constantly create an illusion of transition from one world to another, although he continually turns round in circles (cf. Busby, *23*, p.142, and *24*, passim). From Gauvain's entry into Escavalon onwards, the logic of the narrative is disturbed to such an extent that he can without any sense of surprise arrive at a magic castle where he finds relatives long since dead (cf. Nykrog, *69*, p.270). What I am trying to suggest here is that the narrative of the Gauvain part of *Perceval* largely defies logical analysis (to which the Perceval part had lent itself fairly well).

The Orgueilleuse's change of heart constitutes a kind of exorcism, and she now confesses to Gauvain why she behaved as she did (8927 ff.). When she throws herself on Gauvain's mercy, the roles are reversed as she acquiesces, promising to do as he wishes, just as he had earlier promised her (8972–73). She is now, as Frappier has said, 'délivrée de son lourd secret et d'elle-même' (*33*, p.251).

The following scene in the Castle of Marvels (9005 ff.), with Gauvain sitting on the Marvellous Bed alongside his sister, and the two queens looking on in admiration, is dependent on Gauvain's continued incognito for its effect. He delivers Clarissant's message to Guiromelant, but the latter's suggestion that Clarissant would rather see Gauvain dead than Guiromelant injured in his little toe is considered by her as *folie*. Clarissant's comment and the conversation between the two queens give rise to an explicatory comment by the narrator (9065–73) to the effect that the Eneas-Lavinia comparison is wholly inappropriate, that brotherly and sisterly love is all there will be, and that the mother is in for a surprise. Despite the incomplete state of *Perceval*, there is a certain symmetry about the text as we have it, for Charles Méla has pointed out that whereas the romance opens with the sorrow of Perceval's mother, it breaks off with the joy of Gauvain's (*66*, p.91). There is also a hint of incest present, although few would follow Dragonetti's extensive psychoanalytical interpretation (*28*, pp.212 ff.).

The proposed encounter between Gauvain and Guiromelant and the requirement for witnesses necessitates a conjunction between the world in which Gauvain now finds himself and the Arthurian court. The request to Arthur to come and witness the combat is to be transmitted by one of the *vallets* of the court. Gauvain's instructions to his messenger (9096–134) are character-ised by the same rhetoric and elaborateness already noticed in earlier episodes: he stresses to the lad the importance of silence, reveals his own identity, and urges Arthur and Guenièvre to come with all those present at court. Once more, Gauvain's concern with horses is shown as he ensures that the lad is provided with a suitable mount (9135–37).

The messenger's arrival at Orkney is probably intended by Chrétien to be the beginning of another narrative section. The scene that the messenger finds and that Gauvain had predicted resembles both the beginning of a romance (cf. Schmolke-Hasselmann, *88*) and, more specifically, the earlier scene of Perceval's arrival at Carduel (900 ff.): it is Pentecost, Arthur is in a depressed state because of the absence of Gauvain and faints. As Dame Lore goes to tell Guenièvre of the commotion in the hall, the romance breaks off.

Needless to say, scholars have speculated as to how the romance might have ended: would Perceval and Gauvain have both come to the Grail Castle and met in single combat? Would Perceval have defeated Gauvain? What would have happened to Perceval? And what future is in store for the Arthurian kingdom as a whole? Another intriguing question, put by Per Nykrog, illustrates the nature and extent of the problem: 'But what is going to happen here, when Arthur comes to witness the combat and finds himself face to face with his mother, dead long ago, in the company of Gauvain's mother, who is also dead?' (*69*, pp.269–70). It is tempting, in view of a certain weakness about Arthur and the court, to think that Chrétien was intending to show the superiority of spiritual values over worldly ones, and that he had planned some kind of cataclysmic end for Arthur and the court. One theory has Perceval succeed on a second visit to the Grail Castle (but what is left after achieving the supreme quest?), and Gauvain with Arthur and Guenièvre and the rest sequestrated for ever in the Other World of the Castle of Marvels (cf. Frappier, *33*, p.253). Arguably, there is no need and no justification for assuming such a drastic ending, for there is no real suggestion that Arthurian society and its values are irredeemably evil. It is clear, though, thanks to the Perceval-Gauvain contrast, that Chrétien is offering a commentary on the way of life represented by Gauvain and a prospect of an alternative.

4. Conclusions

Enough parallels and contrasts have been suggested between the Perceval and Gauvain parts of *Perceval* to support the view that Chrétien intended the two sets of adventures to be complementary, and a full commentary on the romance could easily demonstrate that a complex structure is to be discerned. *Perceval* is arguably the romance of Chrétien in which structure and meaning are most inextricably linked.

It is clear in general terms what *Perceval* is about: love, chivalry, religion, and the relationship between them. Chrétien presents his meaning by means of the interplay between the Perceval and the Gauvain adventures. The Gauvain adventures, however, do not simply provide a black and white contrast to those of Perceval, for that would have been simplistic and not in the manner of Chrétien. Rather, episodes and adventures in both parts cast light on each other in different ways: by parallelism, variation, opposition and inversion. Further examples of correspondences between the Perceval and Gauvain parts and within each part are provided by Brand (*21*, passim) and Dragonetti (*28*, p.145). Some of the structuring methods and patterns have also been demonstrated in some detail by Antoinette Saly (*83*, *84*, *85*), who proposes looking at the Gauvain adventures as an oneiric, dreamlike, transformation of those of Perceval: 'Sans doute convient-il de s'interroger sur le *sen* de cette composition romanesque qui ... opérait par métathèse et antithèse des métamorphoses comparables au travail du rêve sur la réalité vécue ou l'activité consciente. Mais ce qui importe le plus avant toute question, c'est de saisir le procédé de fabrication d'un récit qui s'engendre suivant une aussi déconcertante géométrie' (*84*, p.41; cf. also *83*, p.358). The dreamlike status of the narrative has also been stressed by Poirion (*74* and *75*), whilst Nykrog sees it as 'a pioneer's work in the elaboration of a certain narrative form, the literary universe of purely fictional, esthetic romance ... a self-contained world of pure narrative movement and pure playful fantasy' (*69*, p.270). *Perceval* criticism has come a long way since Micha wrote in 1951: 'Il faut aborder le roman [...] sans le revêtir de la couleur de nos rêves, sans reporter sur lui un poids de mystique et de poésie trop lourd pour son assez frêle armature' (*67*, p.122).

Most scholars would agree that generally speaking Chrétien's criticism of Arthurian society leads him to regard Gauvain as a good, but flawed knight. Nevertheless, despite his unorthodox, more pro-Gauvain interpretation, Ribard is of fundamentally the same opinion with respect to the structure of the romance: 'Les deux itinéraires s'éclairent sans doute l'un par l'autre' (*79*, p.108). In a sense, whether Gauvain is living down his past and creating a new identity for himself, as Ribard suggests, may not be crucial to the meaning of the poem. The profane ideal of chivalry needs to be supplemented and completed by spiritual concerns, not destroyed and supplanted. This is what Frappier sees as the difference between *Perceval* and Chrétien's earlier works (*34*, p.216).

In his earlier works, Chrétien had shown how unthinking adherence to customs and convention had caused embarrassment to Arthur, and how the demands of knighthood had caused husbands to neglect their wives. In *Erec et Enide* and *Yvain* he had suggested how *mesure*, a sense of proportion, could enable men and women to co-exist in harmony with each other and society, and in *Yvain* and *Lancelot*, he had hinted that the court was too concerned with itself and the observance of codes of behaviour to retain sight of real human objectives. The general moral to be drawn from his work as a whole is that whilst human behaviour does need to be governed by conventions (*courtoisie* and *chevalerie*), each situation and each relationship requires an individual solution and treatment. When Chrétien comes to cast doubts on the sufficiency of a certain, Arthurian, way of life, it is not surprising that its most illustrious representative, Gauvain, should be shown wanting. But in none of his previous romances, nor in *Perceval*, does Chrétien launch an all-out attack on the values of Arthurian society or its members.

Whilst the system is not perfect, it is not totally inadequate. Leslie Topsfield has aptly remarked that: 'In the Gauvain adventures the whole world may appear to fall apart, yet the centre holds' (*93*, p.298). In the earlier romances, *chevalerie* and *courtoisie* are validated by *amour*, whilst in *Perceval* they are validated as well by *carité*.

The contrastive function of the Gauvain adventures becomes structural in *Perceval* and is the means by which the *san* of the romance is articulated. Perceval's itinerary is more or less linear, and the progress he makes from naïve country lad to courtly lover with prospects of spiritual development is clearly visible. On the other hand, Gauvain is from the outset an established knight at the top of his profession, and he shows no clear change in the course of his lengthy adventures; indeed, his trajectory is circular and fragmented, and he eventually ends up in what seems to be some kind of supernatural imprisonment, although there is no way of telling how permanent it is. Perceval has no past and a future to build, his major obstacle being the sin he committed in causing his mother's death; and however grave the sin, it is clear that it is redeemable. Gauvain has a past that confronts him at every turn: accusations of killing, treason, injustice, are all levelled at him in a constant onslaught. Whereas Perceval is a figure of fun in the early parts of the romance because of his ignorance of the ways of knighthood, the burlesque treatment of Gauvain is Chrétien's manner of saying that even accomplished knighthood can prove inadequate in certain situations. Perceval's love for Blancheflor is a genuine one based on human sympathy and warmth where the reciprocal relationship of love and prowess is visible; Gauvain's contacts with women are either parodic or supernatural, at best fleeting and physical, at worst lustful and squalid.

If most scholars agree on the idea that contrast, parallel and counterpoint between the two major narrative divisions are intentional and a means of discerning Chrétien's purpose, the basic issue is to what extent we are dealing with opposition or complementarity. In the first serious study of *Perceval*, published in 1936 and still basic reading, Wilhelm Kellermann suggested that Chrétien was

intending to show a reconciliation between courtesy and religion
leading to a balanced form of human wisdom (*52*, pp.189 ff.).
Twenty years later, in another important study of Arthurian
romance, Erich Köhler refined Kellermann's suggestion and recast
it in terms of the twelfth-century's own awareness of a real ethical
conflict between *chevalerie* and *clergie* (*55*, p.83). David Fowler, on
the other hand, sees the themes of prowess and charity, undoubtedly
central to the romance, as absolute opposites: 'That these two ideals
were inimical and that charity must ultimately prevail over prowess
together constitute Chrétien's theme' (*32*, p.3). In this view,
Perceval's charity would totally eclipse Gauvain's prowess. Whether
we see these and other concerns in black and white or in various
shades of grey, it is clear that the Arthurian world of *Perceval* is a
troubled one, and that Chrétien's point is social rather than individual (cf. Sturm-Maddox, *91*, p.41).

The real structural principle of *Perceval* is perhaps that of
disruption, which effectively prevents definitive conclusions from
being drawn. Perceval disrupts the lives of his mother, of the Tent
Maiden, of the Chevalier Vermeil, and the peace at Arthur's court.
His failure at the Grail Castle disrupts his own progress and
prolongs the misfortune of the Fisher King and his country. As I
have already suggested, the Gauvain adventures are governed by the
disruption of logic, not only in a narrative sense, but also of the
temporal scheme of the adventures during which the hero encounters members of his own family, some he thinks to be dead, some he
has never seen before, all caught up in a suspension of time. It is
easy to see how this disruptiveness has led scholars to conclude that
Perceval is not only unfinished, but that it also represents a
romance in the early stages of composition. Irrespective of the
strange beauty of the text (which must, of course, remain a subjec-
tive impression), the most telling argument in favour of reading
Perceval as it stands must be that it is difficult to see how any
conventional 'sense' could be made of it at all.

Despite Gerbert de Montreuil's telling us that Chrétien died
before finishing *Perceval*, it is possible that he did not intend to
complete it (after all, he had left the conclusion of *Lancelot* to

Godefroi de Leigni). For Roger Dragonetti (*28*, pp.19–20), the incompleteness is a narrative stratagem and the inconclusiveness part of the *san* of the poem. Of course, we know far too little of the working practices of medieval poets to do other than speculate on this, but that the text breaks off at line 9234 of Roach's edition (with clear demarcations in two of the manuscripts and a change of hand in a third), cleanly, and in full expectation of further developments, suggests something other than mere petering out. Intentional or not, its incompleteness certainly added an extra dimension to the posterity of Chrétien's poem. As with some of Chrétien's other works (notably *Erec et Enide* and *Yvain*), there are foreign adaptations of *Perceval*: the Middle English *Syr Percyvelle of Galles*, the Flemish *Perchevael*, the great Middle High German *Parzival* by Wolfram von Eschenbach, and the two-part Old Norse *Parcevalssaga* and *Valverspattr*. In addition, most of the manuscripts of *Perceval* contain a number of Continuations, amounting in some versions to a compilation of well over 40,000 lines. These Continuations are on the whole fairly loosely attached to Chrétien's poem, and seem to consist of a number of tenuously related adventures featuring Gauvain, Perceval, Caradoc, and Guerrehés (Gauvain's brother), in which the Grail sometimes plays a role, and sometimes does not. They reflect a manner of storytelling that requires further urgent investigation, although here is not the place. In a sense, the medieval view of Chrétien's *Perceval* would have been as part of a much longer work, and it is conceivable that readers of, or listeners to, some of the manuscripts which do not indicate the break at line 9234 might not even have been aware of the transition from Chrétien to the first continuator. Because of its legacy to Western fiction and because of its own often undefinable qualities, Chrétien's *Perceval* has borne out the boast he made at the beginning of his first romance, *Erec et Enide*:

> Des or comancerai l'estoire
> Qui toz jors mes iert en memoire
> Tant con durra crestïantez:
> De ce s'est Crestiiens vantez. (23–26)

Bibliography

TEXTS OF PERCEVAL

1. William Roach (ed.), *Chrétien de Troyes, Le Roman de Perceval ou le Conte du Graal*, Textes Littéraires Français, 71 (Geneva, Droz, 1956; 2nd edn, 1959).
2. Félix Lecoy (ed.), *Les Romans de Chrétien de Troyes édités d'après la copie de Guiot. V: Le Conte du Graal (Perceval)*, Classiques français du moyen âge, 100 and 103 (Paris, Champion, 1972 and 1975).
3. Alfons Hilka (ed.), *Der Percevalroman von Christian von Troyes*, Christian von Troyes *Sämtliche Werke*, V (Halle, Niemeyer, 1932).

TEXTS OF OTHER ROMANCES BY CHRÉTIEN DE TROYES

Foerster's Grosse Ausgabe:

4. Wendelin Foerster (ed.), *Cligès*, Christian von Troyes *Sämtliche Werke*, I (Halle, Niemeyer, 1884).
5. —— (ed.), *Der Löwenritter (Yvain)*, Christian von Troyes *Sämtliche Werke*, II (Halle, Niemeyer, 1887).
6. —— (ed.), *Erec und Enid*, Christian von Troyes *Sämtliche Werke*, III (Halle, Niemeyer, 1890).
7. —— (ed.), *Der Karrenritter (Lancelot) und das Wilhelmsleben*, Christian van Troyes *Sämtliche Werke*, IV (Halle, Niemeyer, 1899).

Roques's Guiot Text:

8. Mario Roques (ed.), *Les Romans de Chrétien de Troyes édités d'après la copie de Guiot. I: Erec et Enide*, Classiques français du moyen âge, 80 (Paris, Champion, 1952).
9. Alexandre Micha (ed.), *Les Romans de Chrétien de Troyes édités d'après la copie de Guiot. II: Cligès*, Classiques français du moyen âge, 84 (Paris, Champion, 1957).
10. Mario Roques (ed.), *Les Romans de Chrétien de Troyes édités d'après la copie de Guiot. III: Le Chevalier de la charrete (Lancelot)*, Classiques français du moyen âge, 86 (Paris, Champion, 1958).

11. Mario Roques (ed.), *Les Romans de Chrétien de Troyes édités d'après la copie de Guiot. IV: Le Chevalier au lion (Yvain)*, Classiques français du moyen âge, 89 (Paris, Champion, 1960).

EDITIONS OF OTHER TEXTS

12. Mary Williams (ed.), Gerbert de Montreuil, *La Continuation de Perceval*, t.I, Classiques français du moyen âge, 28 (Paris, Champion 1922).
13. I.D.O. Arnold and M.M. Pelan (eds), Wace, *La Partie arthurienne du roman de Brut*, Bibliothèque française et romane, série B: textes et documents, I (Paris: Klincksieck, 1962).
14. Sancti Aurelii Augustini Opera, Sect. VI Pars VI, *De Doctrina Christiana Libri quattuor*, recensuit et praefatus est Guilelmus M. Green (Vindobonae, Hoelder-Pichler-Tempsky, 1963).
15. D.W. Robertson, Jr. (trans.), Saint Augustine, *On Christian Doctrine*, The Library of Liberal Arts, 80 (Indianapolis and New York, Bobbs-Merrill, 1958).

STUDIES

This section is extremely selective, given the vast amount of literature Chrétien's poem has generated. I have been particularly selective with regard to works on the origins and development of the Grail legend and the 'interpretations' of the Grail procession in *Perceval*. I have, however, included all studies referred to in the course of this book. Further bibliographical details can be found in R.W. Last and C.E. Pickford, *The Arthurian Bibliography*, 3 vols (Cambridge, D.S. Brewer, 1981, 1983 and 1985), Edmund Reiss, Louise Horner Reiss, and Beverly Taylor, *Arthurian Legend and Literature: an Annotated Bibliography. I: The Middle Ages* (London and New York, Garland, 1984), Douglas Kelly (Bibliography, *53*), and the annual *Bibliographical Bulletin of the International Arthurian Society*.

16. Adolf, Helen, *'Visio Pacis', Holy City and Grail: An Attempt at an Inner History of the Grail Legend* (State College, Pa., Pennsylvania State Univ. Press, 1960).
17. Anitchkof, E., 'Le Saint Graal et les rites eucharistiques', *Romania*, 55 (1929), 174–94.
18. Becker, Ph.- Aug. 'Von den Erzählern neben und nach Chrestien de Troyes', *Zeitschrift für romanische Philologie*, 55 (1935), 385–445.
19. Bezzola, Reto R., *Le Sens de l'aventure et de l'amour (Chrétien de Troyes)* (Paris, La Jeune Parque, 1947).

20. Bloch, R. Howard, *Medieval French Literature and Law* (Berkeley, Los Angeles and London, Univ. of California Press, 1977).

21. Brand, Wolfgang, *Chrétien de Troyes: zur Dichtungstechnik seiner Romane*, Freiburger Schriften zur romanischen Philologie, 19 (Munich: Fink, 1972).

22. Bruckner, Matilda T., *Narrative Invention in Twelfth-Century French Romance: the Convention of Hospitality*, French Forum Monographs, 17 (Lexington, Ky, French Forum, 1980).

23. Busby, Keith, *Gauvain in Old French Literature*, Degré Second, 2 (Amsterdam, Rodopi, 1980).

24. ———, 'Reculer pour mieux avancer: l'itinéraire de Gauvain dans le *Conte du Graal*', in Jacques de Caluwé (ed.), *Chrétien de Troyes et le Graal*, Lettres Médiévales, 1 (Paris, Nizet, 1984), pp.17–26.

25. Colby, Alice M., *The Portrait in Twelfth-Century French Literature: an Example of the Stylistic Originality of Chrétien de Troyes*, Histoire des idées et critique littéraire (Geneva, Droz, 1965).

26. Delbouille, Maurice, 'Genèse du *Conte del Graal*', in *Les Romans du Graal dans la littérature des XIIe et XIIIe siècles* (Paris, CNRS, 1956), pp.83–87.

27. ———, 'Réalité du château du Roi-Pêcheur dans le *Conte del Graal*', in *Mélanges René Crozet* (Poitiers, Société d'Etudes Médiévales, 1966), pp.909–13.

28. Dragonetti, Roger, *La Vie de la lettre au Moyen Age (Le Conte du Graal)* (Paris, Seuil, 1980).

29. Faral, Edmond, *Les Arts poétiques du XIIe et du XIIIe siècle: recherches et documents sur la technique littéraire du moyen âge*, Bibliothèque de l'Ecole des Hautes Etudes, 238 (Paris, Champion, 1924).

30. Foulon, Charles, 'Les Vavasseurs dans les romans de Chrétien de Troyes', in Kenneth Varty (ed.), *An Arthurian Tapestry: Essays in Memory of Lewis Thorpe* (Glasgow, The French Department, 1981), pp.101–13.

31. Fourrier, Anthime, 'Encore sur la chronologie des œuvres de Chrétien de Troyes', *Bibliographical Bulletin of the International Arthurian Society*, 2 (1950), 69–96.

32. Fowler, David C., *Prowess and Charity in the 'Perceval' of Chrétien de Troyes*, University of Washington Publications in Language and Literature, 14 (Seattle, Univ. of Washington Press, 1959).

33. Frappier, Jean, *Chrétien de Troyes et le mythe du graal: étude sur Perceval ou le Conte du Graal* (Paris, SEDES, 1972).

34. ———, *Chrétien de Troyes: l'homme et l'œuvre*, Connaissance des lettres, 50 (Paris, Hatier-Boivin, 1957; 2nd edn, 1968).

35. ——, 'Féerie du château du Roi Pêcheur dans *Le Conte du Graal*', in *Mélanges Jean Fourquet* (Paris, PUF, 1969), pp.101–17.

36. ——, 'Le Graal et ses feux divergents', *Romance Philology*, 24 (1970–71), 373–440.

37. ——, 'Sur la composition du *Conte del Graal*', *Le Moyen Age*, 64 (1958), 67–102.

38. ——, *Autour du Graal*, Publications Romanes et Françaises, 147 (Geneva, Droz, 1977). Includes reprintings of the last four items and other important pieces by Frappier on Grail literature.

39. Freeman, Michelle, 'Jean Frappier et le mythe du Graal', *Œuvres et Critiques*, 5, 2 (1980–81), 129–34.

40. Gallais, Pierre, 'Bleheri, la cour de Poitiers et la diffusion des récits arthuriens sur le continent', in *Moyen âge et littérature comparée: Actes du VIIe Congrès national de Littérature Comparée (Poitiers, 1965)* (Paris, Didier, 1967), pp.47–79.

41. ——, 'Perceval et la conversion de sa famille: à propos d'un article récent', *Cahiers de Civilisation Médiévale*, 4 (1961), 475–80.

42. Gsteiger, Manfred, *Die Landschaftsschilderungen in den Romanen Chrestiens de Troyes: literarische Tradition und künstlerische Gestaltung* (Bern, Francke, 1958).

43. Haidu, Peter, *Aesthetic Distance in Chrétien de Troyes: Irony and Comedy in 'Cligès' and 'Perceval'*, Histoire des idées et critique littéraire (Geneva, Droz, 1968).

44. Haug, Walter, *'Das Land, von welchem niemand widerkehrt': Mythos, Fiktion und Wahrheit in Chrétiens 'Chevalier de la Charrete', im 'Lanzelet' Ulrichs von Zatzikhoven und im 'Lancelot' Prosaroman*, Untersuchungen zur deutschen Literaturgeschichte, 21 (Tübingen, Niemeyer, 1978).

45. Hofer, Stefan, 'La Structure du *Conte del Graal* examinée à la lumière de l'œuvre de Chrétien de Troyes', in *Les Romans du Graal dans la littérature des XIIe et XIIIe siècles* (Paris, CNRS, 1956) pp.15–30.

46. Hoffman, Stanton de V., 'The structure of the *Conte del Graal*', *Romanic Review*, 52 (1961), 81–98.

47. Hoggan, David, 'Le péché de Perceval: pour l'authenticité de l'épisode de l'hermite dans le *Conte du Graal* de Chrétien de Troyes', *Romania*, 93 (1972), 50–76, 244–75.

48. Holmes, Urban Tigner, and Sister M. Amelia Klenke, *Chrétien, Troyes, and the Grail* (Chapel Hill, Univ. of North Carolina Press, 1959).

49. Hunt, Tony, 'The Prologue to Chrestien's *Li Contes del Graal*', *Romania*, 92 (1971), 359–79.

50. ——, 'The Rhetorical Background to the Arthurian Prologue: Tradition and the Old French Prologues', *Forum for Modern Language Studies*, 6 (1970), 1–28.

51. ——, 'Tradition and Originality in the Prologues of Chrestien de Troyes', *Forum for Modern Language Studies*, 8 (1972), 320–44.

52. Kellermann, Wilhelm, *Aufbaustil und Weltbild Chrestiens von Troyes im Percevalroman*, Beihefte zur *Zeitschrift für romanische Philologie*, 88 (Halle, Niemeyer, 1936).

53. Kelly, Douglas, *Chrétien de Troyes: An Analytic Bibliography*, Research Bibliographies and Checklists, 17 (London, Grant & Cutler, 1976). Supplement in preparation.

54. ——, 'Topical Invention in Medieval French Literature', in James J. Murphy (ed.), *Medieval Eloquence: Studies in the Theory and Practice of Medieval Rhetoric* (Berkeley, Los Angeles and London, Univ. of California Press, 1978), pp.230–51.

55. Köhler, Erich, *Ideal und Wirklichkeit in der höfischen Epik: Studien zur Form der frühen Artus- und Graldichtung*, Beihefte zur *Zeitschrift für romanische Philologie*, 97 (Tübingen, Niemeyer, 1956; 2nd edn, 1970).

56. ——, 'Zur Diskussion über die Einheit von Chrestiens *Li Contes del Graal*', *Zeitschrift für romanische Philologie*, 75 (1959), 523–39.

57. ——, 'Le Rôle de la *coutume* dans les romans de Chrétien de Troyes', *Romania*, 81 (1960), 386–97.

58. Lacy, Norris, *The Craft of Chrétien de Troyes: an Essay on Narrative Art*, Davis Medieval Texts and Studies, 3 (Leiden, Brill, 1980).

59. ——, 'Gauvain and the Crisis of Chivalry in the *Conte del Graal*', in Rupert T. Pickens (ed.), *The Sower and His Seed: Essays on Chrétien de Troyes*, French Forum Monographs, 44 (Lexington, Ky, French Forum, 1983), pp.155–64.

60. Le Rider, Paule, *Le Chevalier dans le Conte du Graal de Chrétien de Troyes* (Paris, SEDES, 1978).

61. Loomis, Roger Sherman, *The Grail: from Celtic Myth to Christian Symbol* (Cardiff, Univ. of Wales Press; New York, Columbia Univ. Press, 1963).

62. Luttrell, Claude, *The Creation of the First Arthurian Romance: a Quest* (London, Edward Arnold, 1974).

63. ——, 'The Prologue of Chrestien's *Li Contes del Graal*', *Arthurian Literature*, 3 (1983), 1–25.

64. Marx, Jean, *La Légende arthurienne et le graal*, Bibliothèque de l'Ecole des Hautes Etudes, Section des sciences religieuses, 64 (Paris, Presses Universitaires de France, 1952).

65. Méla, Charles, *Blanchefleur et le saint homme ou la semblance des reliques: étude comparée de littérature médiévale* (Paris, Seuil, 1979).

66. ——, *La Reine et le Graal: la conjointure dans les romans du Graal, de Chrétien de Troyes au livre de Lancelot* (Paris, Seuil, 1984).

67. Micha, Alexandre, 'Le *Perceval* de Chrétien de Troyes (roman éducatif)', in René Nelli (ed.), *Lumière du Graal* (Paris, Les Cahiers du Sud, 1951), pp.122–31.

68. Nitze, William A., *Perceval and the Holy Grail: an Essay on the Romance of Chrétien de Troyes*, University of California Publications in Modern Philology, 28 (Berkeley and Los Angeles, Univ of California Press, 1949).

69. Nykrog, Per, 'Two Creators of Narrative Form in Twelfth Century France: Gautier d'Arras-Chrétien de Troyes', *Speculum*, (1973), 257–76.

70. Olschki, Leonardo, *Il Castello del Re Pescatore e i suoi misteri nel 'Conte del Graal' di Chrétien de Troyes*, Atti dell'Accademia Nazionale dei Lincei, 358, series 8, vol. 10, fascicle 3 (Rome, 1961), pp.101–59. Abridged translation by J.A. Scott as *The Grail Castle and Its Mysteries* (Manchester, Manchester Univ. Press, 1966).

71. Owen, D.D.R., *The Evolution of the Grail Legend*, St Andrews University Publications, 58 (Edinburgh and London, Oliver and Boyd, 1968).

72. Pickens, Rupert T., *The Welsh Knight. Paradoxicality in Chrétien's 'Conte del Graal'*, French Forum Monographs, 6 (Lexington, Ky, French Forum, 1977).

73. ——, 'Le *Conte du Graal (Perceval)*', in Douglas Kelly (ed.), *The Romances of Chrétien de Troyes, a Symposium*, The Edward C. Armstrong Monographs on Medieval Literature, 3 (Lexington, Ky, French Forum, 1985), pp.232–86.

74. Poirion, Daniel, 'L'Ombre mythique de Perceval dans le *Conte del Graal*', *Cahiers de Civilisation Médiévale*, 16 (1973), 191–98.

75. ——, 'Du sang sur la neige: nature et fonction de l'image dans le *Conte du Graal*', in Raymond J. Cormier (ed.), *Voices of Conscience: Essays on Medieval and Modern French Literature in Memory of J.D. Powell and R. Hodgkins* (Philadelphia, Temple Univ. Press, 1976), pp.143–65.

76. Pollmann, Leo, *Chrétien de Troyes und der Conte del Graal*, Beihefte zur *Zeitschrift für romanische Philologie*, 110 (Tübingen, Niemeyer, 1965).

77. Potters, Susan, 'Blood Imagery in Chrétien de Troyes' *Perceval*', *Philological Quarterly*, 56 (1977), 301–09.

78. Ribard, Jacques, 'L'Ecriture romanesque de Chrétien de Troyes d'après le *Perceval*', *Marche Romane*, 25 (1975), 71–81.

79. ——, 'Ecriture symbolique et visée allégorique dans le *Conte du Graal*', *Œuvres et Critiques*, 5, 2, (1980–81), 103–09.

80.   ——, 'Un personnage paradoxal: le Gauwain du *Conte du Graal*', in
      Jacques de Caluwé (ed.), *Lancelot, Yvain et Gauvain*, Lettres Médié-
      vales, 2 (Paris, Nizet, 1984), pp.5–18.

81.   Roach, William, 'Les Continuations du *Conte du Graal*', in *Les
      Romans du Graal dans la littérature des XIIe et XIIIe siècles* (Paris,
      CNRS, 1956), pp.107–18.

82.   ——, 'Le Nom du graal', in *Les Romans du Graal dans la littérature
      des XIIe et XIIIe siècles* (Paris, CNRS, 1956), pp.5–14.

83.   Saly, Antoinette, 'Beaurepaire et Escavalon', *Travaux de linguistique
      et de littérature*, 16,1 (1978), pp.469–81.

84.   ——, 'L'Itinéraire intérieur dans le *Perceval* de Chrétien de Troyes et
      la structure de la quête de Gauvain', in *Voyage, quête, pèlerinage
      dans la littérature et la civilisation médiévales*, *Senefiance*, 2 (Aix-en-
      Provence, CUER MA, 1976), pp.353–61.

85.   ——, 'La Récurrence des motifs en symétrie inverse et la structure du
      Perceval de Chrétien de Troyes', *Travaux de linguistique et de littéra-
      ture*, 21, 2 (1983), 21–41.

86.   Schmid, Elisabeth, *Familiengeschichte und Heilsmythologie: Die
      Verwandtschaftsstrukturen in den französischen und deutschen
      Gralromanen des 12. und 13. Jahrhunderts*, Beihefte zur *Zeitschrift
      für romanische Philologie*, 211 (Tübingen, Niemeyer, 1986).

87.   Schmolke-Hasselmann, Beate, *Der arthurische Versroman von
      Chrestien bis Froissart*, Beihefte zur *Zeitschrift für romanische
      Philologie*, 177 (Tübingen, Niemeyer, 1980).

88.   ——, 'Untersuchungen zur Typik des arthurischen Romananfangs',
      Germanisch-Romanische Monatsschrift, n.s. 31 (1981), 1–13.

89.   Spensley, Ronald M., 'Gauvain's Castle of Marvels Adventure in the
      Conte del Graal', *Medium Aevum*, 42 (1973), 32–37.

90.   Sturm-Maddox, Sara, 'King Arthur's Prophetic Fool: Prospection in
      the *Conte du Graal*', *Marche Romane*, 29 (1979), 103–08.

91.   ——, '"Tenir sa terre en pais": Social Order in the *Brut* and in the
      Conte del Graal', *Studies in Philology*, 81 (1984), 28–41.

92.   Thompson, Albert Wilder, 'The Additions to Chrétien's *Perceval*', in
      Roger Sherman Loomis (ed.), *Arthurian Literature in the Middle
      Ages: A Collaborative History* (Oxford, The Clarendon Press, 1959),
      pp.206–17.

93.   Topsfield, Leslie, *Chrétien de Troyes: a Study of the Arthurian
      Romances* (Cambridge, Cambridge Univ. Press, 1981).

94.   Woledge, Brian, 'Bons vavasseurs et mauvais sénéchaux', in
      Mélanges Rita Lejeune (Gembloux, Duculot, 1969, 1969), t. II,
      pp.1263–77.

CRITICAL GUIDES TO FRENCH TEXTS

edited by
Roger Little, Wolfgang van Emden, David Williams